Alex Bowlby was born in 1924 and educated at Radley. He served with the Greenjackets during World War II, and later joined the 21st S.A.S. (T.A.). Between 1952 and 1956 he wrote advertisements and taught English. In 1957 he began painting. His work has been collected by Ingmar Bergman and exhibited in the Bank of America and in Copenhagen.

In 1969 he published his *Recollections*, in 1974 a novella, *Order of the Day*, and in 1983 a novel, *Roman Candle*. He is currently commissioned to write an account of a key battle in the Italian Campaign.

Alex Bowlby

RECOLLECTIONS OF RIFLEMAN BOWLBY

ITALY, 1944

'All soldiers run away. It does not
matter as long as their supports stand firm.'
att. The Duke of Wellington

ARROW BOOKS

Arrow Books Limited
20 Vauxhall Bridge Road, London SW1V 2SA

An imprint of Random Century Group
London Melbourne Sydney Auckland Johannesburg
and agencies throughout the world

First published in Great Britain by Leo Cooper Ltd 1969
First published in this edition by Leo Cooper Ltd 1989
Arrow edition 1991

Typeset by BookEns Ltd, Baldock, Herts.
Printed and bound in Great Britain by
Cox & Wyman Ltd, Reading, Berkshire

ISBN 0 09 978540 4

To the memory of
Corporals Hardy and Brandon,
Gothic Line, 1944

INTRODUCTION

by John Keegan

Recollections of Rifleman Bowlby belong to the genre of military literature known as 'a voice from the ranks'. But with this difference: Alex Bowlby, though a genuine private soldier, who apparently never aspired to rise above the rank of Rifleman, was a gentleman. He was not, however, one of Kipling's 'gentleman rankers', one of those *déclassé* Victorians who enlisted as a desperate escape from social failure in civilian life. War and conscription took him into the army and, once established in his platoon, he seemed content to share its company and observe and record the experience of fighting an infantryman's war from a worm's eye view. The result, as the thousands of readers who have enjoyed his memoir since it first appeared in 1969 recognize, is one of the most unusual of all books about the British army in the Second World War.

Much of the book's individual flavour is lent it by Bowlby's acute ability to catch and transmit the quality of life in the regiment he belonged to. The '3rd Battalion', as he identifies it, was not an ordinary infantry unit, but part of the Greenjackets, with a high proportion of pre-war regulars in its ranks. Greenjackets – the King's Royal Rifle Corps and the Rifle

Brigade; Bowlby does not tell us which – pride themselves on their independence, the initiative they encourage their N.C.O.s and soldiers to cultivate, and the easy relationship between officers and men. These habits were first developed in the American War of Independence, for which the Greenjackets were raised as skirmishers and sharpshooters, but have been preserved ever since. A final and particular quality is lent to the Greenjackets by the territorial origin of their riflemen. The majority are Londoners, with the Cockney's quick wit, irreverence and street wisdom, all attributes which the Greenjacket spirit fosters.

The battalion which Bowlby joined had spent a long war fighting in the desert as the motorised infantry unit of an armoured division. When he came to it, however, it had transferred to Italy, lost its vehicles and was operating on foot in the hills and valleys of one of the most dangerous battlefields of the Second World War. The German enemy was of high quality – parachutists and panzer grenadiers whom Hitler had rushed to Italy to rescue the German front there after the collapse of the Mussolini régime in August 1943. Such men quickly learnt to exploit the defensive opportunities the Italian landscape offered and to inflict heavy casualties on all Allied soldiers who came against them.

By a quirk Bowlby missed his battalion's worst battle of the campaign, a fight for a little hilltop town in the Gothic Line, called, by the Divisional commander when it was over 'a magnificent failure'. It destroyed most of the company to which he belonged. This episode, though it comes at the end of the book, colours all that he writes about the men with whom he shared the hardships and dangers of the months before. In a sense the book is comedy; but Bowlby's skill is to indicate, from the moment he draws the reader into his narrative, that tragedy lurks at the end. It is this hint of doom lying over all the men to whom he introduces us that lends Rifleman Bowlby's recollections their bitter-sweet quality.

This is certainly not the last time that his book will be re-issued. With half a dozen others, it has become a minor classic of soldiers' memoirs of the British army in the Second World War and will certainly be read as long as that war is remembered.

John Keegan
January 16, 1989

FOREWORD

At the battle of El Alamein a battalion of a rifle regiment was attacked by a Panzer Division. Although caught in unprepared positions it gave no ground and destroyed or crippled fifty-seven tanks. General Montgomery sent a message of congratulations, and subsequent honours included a V.C., a D.S.O., and three D.C.M.s. The action set the seal to the Battalion's Desert reputation. Equipped as a motor-battalion* – one of the original two in the 7th Armoured Division – it had exploited its new role as brilliantly as Sir John Moore's riflemen had exploited theirs. At Sidi Saleh the Battalion had cut round the rear of the retreating Italians, and supported by two batteries of the R.H.A. had held up the entire army. Enemy tanks penetrated as far as Battalion H.Q. before the attack collapsed. The Italian C.-in-C., General Bergonzoli, surrendered to a company commander. For the time being the Italian Desert army ceased to exist. And later, when Rommel swept back through Libya, the Battalion, whose first Desert C.O. was now commanding the Division, formed one of the 'flying columns'

*A mechanized infantry unit whose fighting vehicles – Bren-gun carriers and fifteen-hundredweight trucks – enabled it to operate at a range and speed far beyond that of lorried infantry.

operating behind the enemy lines, ambushing convoys and providing G.H.Q. with some badly needed good news.

Before the last push in Tunisia the 'grapevine' hummed with the rumour that once the campaign ended Montgomery would take the whole of the 8th Army back to England. This went down particularly well with the Rifles. A regular battalion, some two hundred of its men had been abroad since 1937.

Tunisia fell. The Army re-grouped. Whilst the bulk of it received embarkation orders – for Sicily and Salerno, but few knew that till they got there – some units, including the Rifles, were told they were staying in Tunisia.

Rightly or wrongly the bulk of the Rifles felt they were being picked on. The officer in command at the time described their mood as 'restless'. Whilst the Battalion was getting over their disappointment as best they could, they were told that all the 1937 regulars were to return to England under a repatriation scheme. With a stroke of a pen the powers-that-be broke the battalion in two. The returning regulars were as bitter as the men they left behind. Deprived of a frightening proportion of its most experienced troops the Battalion soldiered on. After a spell in Tripoli it moved backwards and forwards between Syria and Egypt, training hard for its next assignment. This turned out to be an unlikely one. In April 1944 some Greek units stationed in and around Alexandria received embarkation orders. For political reasons they declined to obey them. The 3rd was used to disarm the Greeks, and then sent to Italy, along with another battalion of the Rifles, in their place.

On landing at Taranto it was equipped with new vehicles. A fortnight later it made its way to the Adriatic front. Twelve hours before being committed it was ordered to cut across Italy and harbour at Capua, north of Naples. When it reached Capua most of its vehicles were taken away. Italy had suddenly become unsuitable for motor-battalions, and the Battalion was to be used as ordinary infantry.

RECOLLECTIONS OF RIFLEMAN BOWLBY

1

ON THE ROAD

In between Alexandria, where I had joined the Battalion,* and Capua the war-bug got to work. It affected everyone. We were like small boys waiting to play soldiers. And yet as soon as 'D' Company landed it demanded a home-leave. A great crowd of cheering riflemen charged through the olive-grove brandishing sheets of paper and shouting 'Up the Oicks!' The cry was taken up till the whole grove echoed with it. When it stopped there was a great burst of laughter.

'What on earth's happening?' I asked a rifleman.

'The lads want a home-leave before they go into action,' he said. 'They know they won't get it, but it's their way of showing they haven't forgotten Tunis. They're getting up a 'round-robin' to give to the Company Commander.'

The Company Commander received the petition with his usual urbane kindness and 'D' Company got on with the war.

The incident reminded me of the time I saw the 1937 regulars arrive back from North Africa. An hour before they were due all the training-camp's N.C.O.s went to ground. When the regulars arrived I

*To distinguish it from the other two Rifle battalions with whom it was brigaded I shall call it the 3rd Battalion.

1

understood why. The men swarmed on to the square, swinging their belts like clubs, and yelling, 'Where's the fucking R.S.M.! Come out and fight, you fuckers!' It was the healthiest sight I had seen for a long time. I never dreamt that within six months I should be in their Battalion, or that I'd have the luck to land in Mr. Lane's platoon. Most of its riflemen had spent two and three years with the Battalion, and as sailors carry the sea, so they carried the Desert. 'We're an *Alakefak** lot,' they told me, not that I needed telling. Their casual air of independence stuck out a mile. Brown as Arabs they moved with the relaxed assurance of successful poachers. Their accent and wit alone marked them as Londoners. Although they hankered for the Smoke they missed the Desert. Cockney Arabs, with a touch of the sand. Mr. Lane had also been in the Desert. His warmth, dash, and sense of humour made itself felt in whatever the Platoon did. We loved him. Sergeant Meadows and Corporal Baker, M.M., were in support. Meadows, a soft-spoken Scot, used the carrot; Baker, five foot one tall, the stick.

During the first three weeks of May the Battalion prepared to go into action on the Adriatic front. 'D' Company concentrated on route-marches. The Platoon had its own repertoire of songs, 'Lili Marlene' being way out in front. In the Desert the Battalion, in common with other 8th Army units, had made a habit of using captured German weapons against their previous owners, eating any German

---

*Arabic for – literally – 'Happy-go-lucky'. The Platoon laced their talk with Arabic – *Maleesh* ('It doesn't matter') and *Bardin* ('In a little while') were two other favourites – Hindi, and Cockney.

rations that came to hand, and singing 'Lili Marlene'. There's something deeply satisfying about capturing a song, particularly when it's about a girl. Unlike some units who apparently just sung the song in English, leaving it dripping with sentiment, the Battalion had given 'Lili' the works. They had stripped off the schmalz and turned her into a tart who liked it. This was only to be expected from a regiment who had altered the third line of the regimental song, 'England's Glory' so that it went

> 'The Riflemen are going away,
> They won't be back for many a day,
> They've put all the girls in the family way
> To fight for England's Glory.'

We had sung 'Lili' on every march since I had joined the Platoon. We knew it backwards, or we thought we did. On one particular afternoon we were returning to camp after practising a river-crossing. Messing about in boats had turned out to be as delightful as Kenneth Grahame makes it out to be. And lying on the bank watching other people do it was even better. The Platoon celebrated with a tremendous cock-a-hoop 'Lili'. We'd pinched the enemy's song, pinched his girl in a way, and we flung her back at him like a gauntlet. In the middle of the second verse the song got out of control. One moment we were singing it, the next *it* was singing *us*. It took over like an automatic pilot. For the first time in my life I lost all sense of self. I was inextricably part of the Platoon and they were part of me. We were all one. Nothing else mattered. I grinned hugely at my neighbours and they grinned back. In triumph. They'd felt

3

it too. After we'd stopped singing we marched the last hundred yards to the camp in silence. On a route-march we sang and talked and sang again, but not on this one. Everyone had sensed an inexplicable happiness and no one wanted to break the spell. At the time it was a mystery, but a few post-war years of a family *grand-guignol* helped me to unravel it. As I discovered that peace can be a much more disturbing business than war and that the near-loss of one's own sense of self under pressure more terrifying than fear of death in battle I began retreating to memories of the war, and the happiness and security it had brought me. It was then that I suddenly felt I understood what had happened on that march. All of us knew that within a few days we would be in action. Any one of us might be killed. Yet none of us gave it a thought. And because we didn't, because in those great, triumphant shouts we challenged not only the Germans, but the death they stood for, we lost, if only for a moment, the need to protect ourselves. We had let go.

In that last week of May 'D' Company was at its peak. So were the other companies. The feel of the Battalion must have delighted the C.O. The old grudges of Tunis had blown away and the enemy was at hand. The powers-that-be chose this moment to shift the Battalion to the other side of Italy and take away its vehicles. The general who decided that the whole of Italy from Cassino onwards would prove the wrong sort of country for motor-battalions had a case, but it was unfortunate that this official reason for the disbanding of motor-battalions should be quickly followed by a detailed account of an incident that had happened to our own 5th Battalion, who were already operating as a motor-battalion in the Cassino area. A tank-regiment had sent five tanks across a bridge. The bridge came under fire. Three White scout-cars belonging to the 5th followed up the tanks, but the leading vehicle got knocked out in the middle of the bridge. The remaining two Whites withdrew. The tanks across the bridge reported they were being attacked by bazookas. The tank C.O. asked for the 5th's scout-cars to cross the bridge so that their crews could deal with the bazookas. The 5th's C.O. said that the shell-fire was too heavy. Whilst they were arguing the bazookas knocked out all five tanks. The Divisional General happened to be a tank man. As far as our battalion was concerned one motorized balls-up had cost us our vehicles. The 1st Battalion lost theirs too. But not the 5th. They were to still operate as a motor-battalion. This infuriated us. Apart from being responsible for the shake-up the 5th was a territorial Battalion with less than a year's battle experience and nothing much to show for it. They had been in the Division longer than the other two battalions, hence their privilege. 'That bloody shower!' was the 3rd's way of describing the 5th. A wit amended this to 'the Mobile Bath-unit'. The name stuck.

After immediate regimental pressure the 3rd and 1st were allotted more Bren carriers than the normal infantry establishment. The motor-companies ceased to exist. Instead of four fifteen-hundredweights a platoon there was one. Drivers and mechanics became ordinary riflemen, and R.A.S.C. three-tonners took the place of the fifteen-hundredweights. There was something *infra dig* about being carried by the Service Corps. Men who had fought their way all over Africa had developed a keen sense of independence and one-upmanship. This was destroyed overnight. In the Battalion re-organizations that followed Mr. Lane went to a carrier platoon. We did our best to accept this as just one of those things.

The Battalion arrived at Capua on May 25th. From then onwards it was at twenty-four hours to move operationally. Cassino had fallen on the 11th, the Adolf Hitler line on the 25th. The Division was waiting to exploit the break-through. On the 28th we got the wire. We were moving off at 8 a.m. the following day.

The prospect of action roused the Platoon. And I had something else to get excited about. It happened to be my twentieth birthday, and when the post-corporal arrived with the Platoon's mail eight out of twelve letters were for me, along with a pound of Dunhill's 'Royal Yacht'. After I had had four letters in a row there was an outcry. When I explained there were shouts of 'Sweet seventeen, and never been kissed!' and 'Leave 'im alone, 'e's a big boy now.' (This from Corporal Baker.) The parcels did it. I burst out laughing and didn't stop till I reached my bivouac. Who could have had a better start to a birthday? After reading my mail I lay down under an olive-tree, and filled my favourite pipe. This had caused something of a sensation. Its size and shape had drawn comparisons with a two-inch mortar, a saxaphone, and a lavatory bowl. To me it had become a talisman. As I lit it a piece of raw tobacco fell in my eye. The pain was explosive. I leapt to my feet and clapping both hands to the eye ran round in circles. My performance mystified the Platoon – 'What's he at?' they shouted – until Sergeant Meadows caught hold of me, and found out. Whilst he removed the tobacco Corporal Baker remarked that when the Germans saw my pipe they'd 'pack it in'.

We spent the rest of the day packing stores and equipment. Everything except our bedding and mortar-bombs, which were to travel on the fifteen-hundredweight, along with Sergeant Meadows, was stowed on the three-tonner. We then practised getting on board ourselves. We needed to. The first time we tried it only half the Platoon could squeeze in. After a lot of re-packing all twenty-four of us made it.

That night I sat outside my bivouac chatting to O'Connor, a thirteen-stone publican from County Cork (by way of Shoreditch). He gave the impression of being as firmly rooted as the trees around him, a comforting one just then.

'The first time you were in action, Paddy, were you afraid of running away?' I asked him.

O'Connor chuckled.

'Yerrah, I'd say!'

'Did you feel afraid of being afraid?'

'Now don't start worrying, Alec. I'll look after you.'

'It's funny, you know. I feel excited and afraid at the same time.'

'You'll be all right.'

We grinned at one another.

O'Connor turned in, suggesting I do the same, but for some time I sat looking at the stars, trying to find an answer.

First thing in the morning O'Connor went to

7

scrounge some tea from the cooks. He ran back shouting 'They buggered off! Ernie Cross and Joe Bates. Them and three others!'

O'Connor enjoyed the incredulous shouts of 'No!' (Cross had been my section-commander, and Bates had also belonged to it) then added: 'They took a three-tonner full of food and petrol with them!'

Everyone laughed except Baker. When Rifleman Cooper shouted 'Good luck!' Baker snapped his head off.

'Turn it up, Titch,' said Cooper defensively. 'If they've 'ad enough now's the time to pack it in.'

'We'd be well there if everyone said that!'

'Sammy's right,' said Phillips. 'Better it 'appens now than in the Line.'

'Better it 'appens nowhere!' said Baker.

O'Connor had the last word, as usual.

'Yerrah,' he said. 'I bet the C.O.'s doing his nut!'

The desertion of Cross and Bates reminded me of the times I had just avoided a beating at school whilst others hadn't. I had the same guilty feeling of excitement. The ethics of desertion had a deeper pull. They were so unexpected.

During breakfast a Corporal Swallow arrived to take over command of my section. He had never been in action and the Desert men knew it. His barrack-room style of giving orders cut no ice with them. They just grinned. Swallow blushed.

When the Platoon boarded the three-tonner Humphreys came into his own. He and two others who had just joined the Battalion had belonged to a 1st Army unit, and had come in for some heavy ribbing from the Desert men. Humphreys thrived on it.

He wore his beret as if he were still wheeling a barrow, and one look at his face made you want to laugh. When the three-tonner began revving-up he let fly a tremendous 'Moo!' As we moved off 'Moos!' and 'Baa-ahs!' were passing down the length of the company, and on into the next. This delighted us.

The Battalion joined the Brigade convoy, which joined the Divisional convoy, which joined a Corps convoy; the result was reputed to be twenty miles long. Its official speed was 8 m.p.h., the actual one nearer 5 m.p.h. The main roads had been mined and, nose to tail, we meandered up country lanes. These were picketed with warning notices of 'Dust is Death – watch your dust', the enemy being in the habit of shelling dust clouds. We watched our dust all right. The gap between the three-tonner's tarpaulin and the tailboard sucked it up like a vacuum cleaner. We let down the flap-end of the tarpaulin but lack of air soon made us open it again. We tried taking the tarpaulin off altogether – an awkward job on the move. This stopped the vacuum. It also exposed us to the effects of sun-glare on steel and the blinding white-ness of the dust. We replaced the tarpaulin. The dust poured in. At times we couldn't see across the truck. And whenever we halted the sun got just that bit more grip on the tarpaulin. By midday the heat was worse than the dust. We lay around in sticky lumps, too exhausted to even speak.

In the afternoon the convoy moved on to a road. At the first halt someone suggested brewing up. The Platoon sprang to life. One man filled a cut-down biscuit-tin with petrol, another filled the brew-can. The water boiled in less than thirty seconds. A packet

9

of tea, half a tin of evaporated milk, and handfuls of sugar produced a brew of right colour and consistency. Most of us ate our bully – we had a tin each – and biscuits, but Humphreys opened his emergency rations as well. This was a tin of concentrated chocolate marked 'Not to be opened except by order of an officer.' Humphreys read the instructions out loud, then opened the tin, remarking, 'Makes it taste better, don't it.'

After this I fell asleep, waking up in time to see a difference between Coke and Humphreys. Coke was a hard case. He invariably looked as if he had just heard the worst possible news, and his flattened, yellow features didn't soften the blow. Nor did his methods of looking after Number One. He had seen to it that he was first on to the three-tonner, so as to secure the most comfortable position, up against the stores in the depth of the truck. This hadn't proved as luxurious as he had hoped, and using his size eleven boots like two tanks he set about moving house. Ignoring his neighbours' curses he wriggled around until he found the right spot for his back, bottom, and legs. His boots ended up on Humphreys's legs. Humphreys was asleep, or appeared to be. When Coke showed no signs of moving his boots Humphreys opened one eye.

'Do us a favour, Cokey, will you?' he said. 'Just move your flipping boots!'

Coke sneered at him.

'Where do you think you are?' he said. 'The back parlour?'

Humphreys sat up quickly, and flicked Coke's feet on to the floor.

'Watch it,' said Coke, without conviction.

10

Humphreys laughed; it was an extraordinary sound, like someone swallowing soup. There was no answer to it. Humphreys looked round for another victim, and spotted Page asleep by the tailboard. Leaning forward he dug him in the ribs. Page jumped. 'What's up!' he said.

'We're surrounded!' hissed Humphreys. ''Ordes of 'em!'

Page grinned.

'You wouldn't be 'ere if we was,' he said.

Humphreys examined Page's face as if it caused him pain.

'What an 'orrible face you've got, Page! Why don't you go and 'ide your 'orrible face?'

Page leered back at him.

''Orrible 'Umphreys, why don't you go and get your 'orrible knees brown.'

This was a nice piece of impudence, Page being a year younger than myself, and as much of a rookie. But Humphreys replied by switching targets.

'Anyone like 'arf a bully sandwich?' he asked invitingly.

'Yeah, I would, Barney,' said Gibson, who had been at Dunkirk, and hadn't quite recovered from it.

'So would I,' said Humphreys.

Everyone laughed except Gibson.

'You blooming First Army wallahs!' he yelled. 'You want to get some sand in your 'air!'

Humphreys took this on his glove.

'Don't give us that,' he said. 'All you Eighth Army blokes did was brew-up. It took a real army to sock old Rommel.'

They howled him down with 'Come off it!', 'Get

your knees brown!' and 'You couldn't punch pussy!'
O'Connor chuckled noisily, and I knew the big stuff
was coming.

'Yerrah?' he said. 'I'll never forget the time we took
some prisoners in Tunisia. They told us they were
waiting for the Eighth Army, as they didn't want to
surrender to boys!'

Page chipped in on the laughter.

'Why don't you blokes turn it up?' he said. 'You
know you 'ad to wait for real soldiers like me and old
Alec to win the war for you.'

This brought the house down.

In the late afternoon we passed through the outskirts
of Cassino. Tanks and carriers lay around like burnt
tins on a rubbish heap. A row of black crosses,
topped with coal-scuttle helmets, snatched our pity.
The smell – the sour-sweet stench of rotting flesh –
cut it short. Instinctively I realized I was smelling my
own kind, and not animals. I understood what they
must feel in a slaughter-house. These dead were
under the rubble. If we could have seen their bodies
it would have helped. The unseen, unconsecrated
dead assumed a most terrifying power. Their protest
filled the truck. We avoided one another's eyes.

After a hot meal – a dispatch-rider delivered some
vacuum flasks containing stew, rice pudding and tea
– we settled down for a night on the road. We were
all prepared to lump it – all except Coke. He shifted
himself about like a dog with fleas, and the men near
him got little sleep. At dawn the convoy negotiated
an exceptionally bumpy diversion, leaving the road
and crossing a series of half-filled mine-craters. The
truck bucked like a steer. A rifle lodged in the roof of

12

the truck, in between the framework and the tarpaulin, fell – on to Coke's foot. The Platoon cheered loudly.

After breakfast – porridge and bacon, as usual – Humphreys had a brief patter with Page, then turned his attention to Coke, who was looking sourer than ever.

''ad kittens yet, Cokey boy?' he asked him.

'Why don't you get stuffed!' said Coke.

'What, and look like you?'

Coke glowered at him.

'Don't look at us like that, Cokey! You're bad for me 'eart, you are!'

'You've got more mouth than a cow's got cunt!'

'Naughty, naughty!' said Humphreys, and looking up at the tarpaulin he began singing:

> 'Get away, you dirty bastard,
>   Get away from me!
> I ain't no prairie flower,
>   I ain't no rose!
> Keep off my nasal organ,
>   Keep away from me!
> If you want a bit o' bum,
>   You can have my chum,
> But you'll get fuck all from me!'

Humphreys then turned towards the tailboard and shielding his eyes peered dramatically at nothing.

'There they be, pard!' he shouted at Page. 'Them varmint Indians again!'

Crooking his finger he leant out over the tailboard and went 'Boom! Boom! Boom!' Page followed suit. The performance ended with Humphreys shouting, 'And another Redskin bit the dust!'

13

Soon after this the convoy struck the dustiest lane yet. In the thick of it, when we couldn't see one another for dust, Humphreys shouted, 'How's this suit you sandy-haired shite-hawkes!'

Back on the road we halted for the umpteenth time. We had just decided we could not afford another brew until later in the day when Sergeant Meadows looked in on us.

'De-bus, lads,' he said quietly. 'There's some German paratroopers about, and the convoy may be attacked.'

For a moment no one moved. The paratroopers' defence of Cassino was still fresh in our minds. Nobody wanted to meet *them*.

'All right, lads!' shouted Baker. 'Let's have you!'

The Platoon piled out of the truck and took up positions on either side of the road. I was anxiously peering through a gap in a hedge when I heard someone running down the road. It was a R.E.M.E. sergeant brandishing a Tommy-gun swathed in flannelette.

'For Christ's sake show me how it works!' he yelled. 'I've never fired the bloody thing!'

We all burst out laughing. The Sergeant halted uncertainly. Sergeant Meadows took the gun off him, unwrapped it, and showed him how it worked.

This snapped the tension. We were no longer worried about paratroopers. If they came, they came. In the meanwhile we began reading some leaflets scattered in the ditches. (The Germans made a point of shelling their line of retreat with propaganda.) These were crude, in both senses. One had an illustration of a G.I. lifting a girl's skirt underneath a tree. Humphreys read the 'story' out loud, with appropriate gestures.

'This is a true account of what happened to an innocent girl from Maidstone who met an American.' (At this point Humphreys assumed a falsetto): 'One night I was walking home when an American soldier asked me if he could accompany me. Not knowing Americans ("Much!" said Humphreys, in his normal voice) I said yes. On the way he pointed to some bushes and said there was a lovely view from them. We went over and sat down. He opened a can of beer and after he had had a drink he pulled me into the bushes, inned me and outed me, wiped his tallywock on my skirt, pissed in the beer, and walked away whistling "God Save the King." '

We had a belly-laugh at this. I wished the author could have heard us. As it was we began collecting the leaflets, as one collects stamps. Humphreys and I were contesting a juicy-looking specimen when it tore in two. As we glared at one another Sergeant Meadows shouted, 'O.K., lads! On the truck! False alarm!'

We clambered on board, talking noisily, and the convoy moved on.

2
THE NIGHT ATTACK

Later that day the Company left the main convoy, and wandered off by itself. The enemy were thought to have abandoned a particular mountain; we were to make sure they had.

We climbed the mountain, found that the enemy had pulled out, and climbed down again next morning. The exercise gave us a glimpse of things to come. The view from the top of the mountain was – mountains. There seemed no end to them.

Towards evening we harboured next to a battery of 3·7s. 'Dig in,' we were told. After completing a 'minimum' trench – eighteen-inch deep, body-length – I settled down for a nap. The gunners opened up with a barrage that lasted three hours. I slept right through it.

Our next move – at 2 a.m. – took us into the mountains. As I tumbled sleepily out of the three-tonner I saw the dawn. It was breaking over the mountains, pale yellow over jet-black. I had never seen anything so beautiful. The yellow changed to pink, the pink to orange and then Swallow tapped me on the shoulder.

'Report to the C.S.M. with a spade,' he said.

I knew what *that* meant.

The C.S.M. had picked out a soft piece of ground but I didn't appreciate it. This was the second day running Swallow had detailed me for a latrine fatigue.

'Working up an appetite?' shouted Baker.

He came over and listened to me letting off steam.

'And to think of all the money your pa spent on your education,' he said. 'Then you end up with us lot. Still, that's what comes of being a capitalist. Your pa earned 'is pile inching pennies off blind men and swiping the jam off the kiddies' bread. So it serves you right.'

I had heard the 'jam and pennies' part before, but it still made me laugh. Satisfied with my change in mood Baker sat down.

'You 'eard Swallow's latest?' he said. ''e's trying to take over platoon sergeant.'

Apparently Swallow had discovered that he was senior corporal in the Platoon, Baker's M.M. and battle experience counting for nothing, and had told Sergeant Meadows that he, Swallow, ought to be acting platoon sergeant in place of Baker. Meadows had persuaded him not to press his claim for the time being, but there was nothing to prevent Swallow eventually taking over unless, of course, the Platoon received a new officer. It was rough on Baker.

The harbour's setting – a cross between the Cotswolds and the West Highlands – put the Company in holiday mood. The discovery of a neighbouring torrent made the day. The touch of that ice-cold water is something I've never forgotten. I splashed around like a child, laughing at the way the water swept between my legs, then plunged under, shedding all the dust and stickiness in one ecstatic thrust. Afterwards I lay on the bank with O'Connor and Cooper without a care in the world. The sun soon dried us, and we began stuffing one another's mouths with grass. Cooper had a warmth and gentleness that he expressed almost entirely with his eyes. When I was with him words no longer had the same – over-rated – value. Tiring of grass-stuffing we watched the rest of the Company in the water. Their nakedness had a timeless quality. Argonauts at play.

Swallow was waiting for us at the harbour.

'There's a company orders group on,' he told us. 'A platoon one's coming up.'

He returned from this at his most pompous.

'Tonight,' he said, 'the Company is to attack a village five miles the other side of this hill. It is thought that the remaining enemy, estimated at between thirty and forty strong, are pulling out tonight, and our object is to get there before they do.'

'Sod that!' said Gibson. 'Why can't we let them get out first?'

The section tittered.

'Those are the orders!' snapped Swallow. 'And no more funny stuff!'

'All right, matey, don't do your nut,' said Gibson, giving me a sly grin.

Swallow opened up a large-scale map and showed us the village – it was on top of a hill – and the route we were to take. I was glad I wasn't leading the way.

'The trucks will take us to a start-line a mile from the village,' continued Swallow. 'We will rendezvous with "A" Company, who will occupy the hill on our left. The order of march is Four Platoon, Five, Six

18

and H.Q. We shall be leading section of the Company.'
(There were groans at this.) 'Each rifleman will carry
a pick or shovel, two hundred rounds of ammo., two
grenades, and four Bren magazines. Steel helmets
will be worn. So will greatcoats – in bandolier style.
Small-packs, gas-capes, and entrenching* tools will
be carried in the usual way. Make sure you fill your
water-bottles. The Platoon will start getting dressed
at 20.00 hours. We move off at 20.45 hours, and
should be in the village by midnight. Any questions?'

'Yerrah,' said O'Connor. 'When's mangiare up?'

'In half an hour!' said Swallow, glaring at O'Connor
as if he wanted to lecture him on the sort of question
he ought to have asked.

After supper I slipped off by myself. The mountains
I had watched at dawn had their colours now – deep-
sea greens and greys, and stipples of red earth. They
were comfortable mountains, ones you could live
with. Time had worn away their teeth. There
remained a soft beauty, an indefinable air of benevo-
lence. As I looked at them I remembered the Chinese
philosophers who lived in the mountains and who
did nothing except watch the dawn and sunset. How
right they were. What would they have made of us?
To rub in the irony everything was absolutely quiet.
You couldn't hear a voice, let alone a gun. The war
might have been a hundred miles away. I thought of
the Germans in the village and wondered if they
were thinking the same.

When I returned the Platoon were dressing for the
attack. The greatcoats were hell.

*A hatchet-like instrument in two pieces.

19

'This is 'ow the poor sods dressed in the last war, ain't it?' said Page.

'Well, I 'ope they don't think they're still fighting the same fucking war,' said Humphreys, giving his coat a vicious thump.

One or two of the Desert men were old hands at the game, and went round fixing the coats. Time was getting short so I tried to finish mine by myself. The result looked like a pantomime sausage. When I draped it round me the Platoon stopped to watch.

'Send for the midwife, Charlie!' yelled Humphreys.

Baker provided the equivalent, after a provisionary 'If your pa could see you now!' He then shoved a pick between the small of my back and my haversack, and hung pouches of Bren magazines round my neck.

'Blooming Christmas trees!' muttered Gibson.

O'Connor took me on one side.

'Remember, Alec,' he said. 'Keep your nut down. Death or glory boys don't last.'

I appreciated the advice, although there didn't seem any danger of my breaking it. I was more concerned about not running away. The mixture of fear and excitement I had felt the night before we left Capua intensified. It was like sitting in a boxing-ring, waiting for the bell.

We left harbour at dusk. The trucks drove without lights, and we took nearly two hours to cover five miles. When we dismounted it was so dark we could hardly see one another. Swallow went to look for Sergeant Meadows. When he came back he pointed vaguely into the darkness, and said, 'The village is up there. We're starting right away.'

I had always imagined that all real attacks would go like clockwork, and had wondered how I would fit in. Not being able to even see the hill our objective was on made me feel more confident.

The section lined up in single file. Sergeant Meadows had a word with each of us, cracked a joke, then led us into a field. Half-way across I saw a wall. The hill was behind it. We went through a gap in the wall and into a strip of olive-trees. Behind them was another wall. We were at the foot of a terrace. The novelty appealed to me. I hadn't heard of a night attack up an olive terrace.

All went well until the fourth wall. Sergeant Meadows halted very suddenly. The section piled gently into one another, like dodgems in slow motion.

'The bloody path's finished!' whispered Meadows.

We hunted round for another. There wasn't one. We had to climb the walls. In daylight and without extra equipment this would have been easy. As it was we couldn't pick the rotten foothold and the weight of equipment destroyed any sense of balance. The section managed the first wall without a spill. O'Connor was half-way up the second when he fell on top of me. Together we knocked Gibson flat. The three of us rolled in a heap, laughing and swearing. Swallow hissed at us to be quiet. He then ticked off O'Connor for being clumsy. At the next wall Swallow fell off himself. I cheered silently.

As we gained height we heard the rest of the Company crashing after us. They sounded like elephants in the jungle. The sound must have carried for miles. We looked at one another and laughed out loud. There would be no Germans in the village.

21

How could there be, when the advance was only fit for the Marx Brothers? But the farce soon lost its edge. At one wall I fell off three times. If we fell on our backs, which we invariably did, the weight and placing of our equipment made it almost impossible to get up by ourselves. We floundered around like unhorsed knights until someone on their feet helped us up. Once over a wall we lay on our side, getting our breath back, and wiping the sweat off our faces – not being able to do this whilst climbing proved infuriating. The slow-running rivulets on either side of my nose felt like crawling flies.

We had one five-minute rest. The agony of starting up again ruled out any more. We paused only for breath, and to adjust equipment. Some of mine was beyond hope. The pick-helve had rubbed the back of my neck raw, my bayonet-scabbard tripped me on the terraces – as if the walls weren't enough – and my steel helmet kept falling over my eyes. This I took in my fall, as you might say. But not the Bren magazines. Utility pouches consist of two pouches linked by a strip of webbing. The only place to wear them is round your neck. They hung round mine like pendulums in a gale. The weight of the magazines – ten pounds – forced my chin on to my chest. As I walked they yanked at my neck. I cursed them aloud. They yanked back.

We blundered on, lost in our own particular nightmares, until a word from Meadows drew us together.

'There's a *casa* up here,' he whispered. 'There may be some Teds* inside. Come up and cover me whilst

*Short for *Tedeschi*, Italian for 'Germans'.

I have a dekko.'

The house stood in a small clearing. Meadows walked up to the front door. He paused uncertainly, then knocked. Somebody scuffled away from the other side of the door. The section released safety-catches. Meadows knocked again. No sound this time. As Meadows put an ear to the door, O'Connor strode forward and put his rifle-butt through a window. Screams of *'Mamma mia! Mamma mia!'* blasted the night. We grinned with relief.

'Inglesi,' said Meadows, and as the noise died down led us across the clearing.

We climbed one more wall. Instead of a terrace we saw a road ending in the village. We had a hundred yards to go. An untimely moon emphasized the lack of cover. There wasn't even a hedge to creep along, not that it worried us. We were too busy drinking from our water-bottles. At a sign from Meadows we advanced once more. It was some advance. We lurched along like drunks returning home. I didn't care if the Germans were in the village. If they shot me, they shot me. They could have the Bren mags. instead. Nobody shot us, but as we entered the village a man stole out of the shadows.

'Inglesi? Tedeschi?' he asked cautiously.

'Inglesi,' said Meadows.

'Aaah, *Inglesi! Inglesi!'*

The shadows turned into a mob of cheering villagers. Women kissed everyone they could lay hands on. I wasn't in the mood. Nor was O'Connor. We retreated to a parapet overlooking the valley. Loosening my belt I smashed the magazines against the wall. That made me feel much better. Leaning

23

against it myself I surveyed the liberation. This was just as it should be. No Germans. No fighting. Then I heard a rustle. Right behind me. Before I could turn someone pinioned my arms. As I stiffened with shock a voice bellowed '*Inglese, amico*! *Amico, Inglese*!' and the owner began kissing me on both cheeks. He had a stubble of beard, and liked garlic. He was also very strong. He hugged me like a bear, alternating '*Inglese, amico*!' with kisses until he ran out of breath. He then released me, and stood there waiting for *me* to start. Still half-dazed I just said 'Amico'. 'Brava!' shouted the Italian and thumping me on the back ran off to join the rest of the villagers. I flopped down by the parapet. O'Connor was already there and laughing so much he couldn't speak. I glared at him reproachfully, then began laughing myself, and went on till it hurt.

The villagers had brought out demi-johns of wine. Baker ran round telling the Platoon not to drink any. The Platoon pulled out their mess-tins. I saw Humphreys get a tinful of wine, only to have Baker snatch it out of his hand. As Baker moved on so Humphreys produced his other mess-tin. The villager filled that, Humphreys murmuring '*Buono*! *Buono*!' The climax came when Cooper began to walk away with a villager.

'Where the 'ell do you think you're going?' yelled Baker.

"e's asked me in for supper,' said Cooper innocently.

For a moment Baker was speechless.

'What do you think this is?' he said, finally. 'A picnic? Come back 'ere before I do my nut!'

Cooper rejoined the Platoon, who were now sharing

cigarettes with the villagers. There's something cosy about cigarettes in the dark. As I watched their glow I decided they added the finishing touch to the attack. It had been more of a pushover than I dared hope.

'Sergeant Meadows?' said the voice of the Company Commander.

'Sir?'

'Will you take your Platoon, and dig in on the slope outside the village?'

Baker ran round like the sheep-dog collecting its flock.

'Corporal Newton, get your section cracking!' he shouted. 'Coke, come 'ere! Humphreys, put that fag out!'

The Platoon formed up in threes near Major Dunkerley. 'Why did 'e 'ave to come and spoil the fun?' groaned Humphreys. 'Same old story,' said Phillips, the Platoon's Cassandra. 'H.Q. inside. Us poor sods in the open.' Baker told us to stop nattering, then marched the Platoon out of the village. The slope was uninvitingly bare. Meadows picked out section positions and we began digging in. Nobody bothered to use picks or shovels. We just tickled the turf with our entrenching tools.

'This reminds me of the Desert,' said O'Connor, thoughtfully. 'I'll never forget it. Major Henderson was in command of the Company. We'd just harboured for the night —'

O'Connor was interrupted by a 'whooshing!' noise overhead. As we looked up we heard two more. Something exploded in the valley.

'Mortars!' said O'Connor.

We got down on our knees and really dug. A bomb

25

landed in the village. Another burst at the top of the slope. I threw myself flat. Shrapnel whirred overhead. The sound struck home. It was comparatively slow-moving. Instead of the brief shock of an explosion it caused a terrifying build-up of tension, an 'it's-going-to-get-you' feeling. My heart beat as if I'd just run a hundred yards.

A clutch of bombs straddled the Platoon. I waited for the screams.

'Is everyone all right?' shouted Meadows.

Somehow or other everyone was. Getting to my knees I dug for my life. I dug until my forearms ached so much I sobbed. Then a bomb burst almost in my face. The flash was white-hot. I lay on the ground half-stunned.

'Are you all right, Alec? Are you all right?'

O'Connor sounded as if he were speaking through a tunnel. I shook my head, hoping to hear better, and told him I was all right, just a bit deaf.

The after-effects of the near-miss proved unexpectedly soothing. It was rather like having a touch of anaesthetic. I felt too hazy to be afraid. In between explosions I heard the Company Commander on the field-telephone. The words 'counter-barrage' had a comforting ring about them. But when our guns opened up they fired at the mountain *behind* us. Nothing Major Dunkerley said – and he said plenty – altered this. Several hundred shells landed just where the enemy weren't.

By the time my haziness had worn off the enemy had switched his fire on to the village. We heard women screaming, and our medical orderlies ran off to help with the wounded.

Every now and again the odd bomb landed on the slope. The worst thing about mortar-bombs is their silence. You can't hear the damn things coming. The one that had nearly got me had made no noise until it had exploded. Once I heard a 'whoosh!', and flung myself flat, only to realize that it was O'Connor blowing his nose.

The mortaring stopped around three o'clock. The Company had had no casualties. Although I relaxed, I didn't fall asleep. I didn't fancy being woken up by a bomb. Instead I drifted into a deeply satisying semiconsciousness, aware of voices and movements, yet remaining snugly relaxed in a world of my own. It had all the advantages of sleep, with none of the disadvantages; I relished every moment of it.

Shortly after dawn the Company was ordered to withdraw. As we marched down the road there was a fall of dew. I had never realized dew actually fell, and the discovery delighted me.

3

'THIS IS NOTHING'

We rejoined the Divisional convoy later that morning –
June 2nd. The Indians looked like winning the 'Rome
stakes'. We were out of the race, third division in
reserve, moving through a backwash of dead Germans,
dead horses, and wrecked gun-carriages. We could
tell from their injuries and from the state of the road
– pock-marked with shell-holes – that they had been
caught in a barrage. We stared about us in silence.
What had once been man was now a bundle of rags.
'There but for the grace of God' must have been in
all our thoughts, and yet the bodies seemed curiously
remote, as if they had nothing to do with us, and
never had. They had none of the horror of the
unseen dead. All the same I was glad when Gibson
broke the silence by remarking that if the Germans
were using horses they must be in a bad way.

In the afternoon we had a brew-up with a difference.
Phillip's face alone prophesied disasters – O'Connor
said it was because he had been a fishmonger, and
had had to handle iced fish before breakfast – but
when they came he knew how to cope. He and
Cooper had just lit the petrol when the convoy began
moving. Cooper went to dowse the flame. Phillips
stopped him. An awed Platoon watched the pair

stand their ground until the tea was made. By then we were fifty yards ahead, and still moving. Holding the brew-can between them they ran gingerly after us, keeping one eye on the tea. We cheered like mad. They made the truck without spilling a drop.

This particular stretch on the road lasted forty-eight hours. Life in a truck lost its charm. Apart from the occasional 'shop' – the non-existence of the Luft-waffe for example – we were only interested in meals and brewing-up. By the morning of June 4th we began wondering if we would ever harbour again. When someone shouted 'We're turning off the road!' we reacted like shipwrecked sailors spotting smoke.

The Company pulled into a large field surrounded by ripening corn, and backed by a semicircle of hills.

'We're here for twenty-four hours,' said Meadows, pausing to acknowledge our cheers. 'And Mr. Simmonds has arrived to take over the Platoon.'

We cheered again (Mr. Simmonds had commanded the Platoon in Tunisia, and had been second-in-command of the Company in Egypt and Taranto).

Swarming off the truck we ran over to the fifteen-hundredweight to get our bed-rolls. Like everyone else I had a 'Desert bed' – a tight-fitting, ready-to-wear cocoon of blankets. I was soon in it. 'Ginger', our R.A.S.C. driver, took it into his head to have a shave. Even Swallow wasn't *that* keen.

'Oi, Ginger!' shouted Gibson. 'You after a stripe, or something?'

'Ginger' continued to work up an enormous lather. His enthusiasm made bed all the more comfortable. As I watched him I heard a curious rushing noise, followed by an explosion. I sat up. So did the rest of the section. Two more explosions, then a third, much closer. Hot air hit me in the face.

'We're being shelled!' I yelled.

We struggled out of our blankets. It looked like some sort of sack-race. As I got clear I saw a dud shell land at the foot of the Platoon's dispatch-rider. It showered him with red dust. The D.R. ran on, his face white beneath the dust. I raced for the ditch he was already in. Tripping on the edge I went into it head first. As I picked myself up I heard a familiar chuckle.

'How's it going, Alec?' said Baker.

I grinned back at him. There was no one I would sooner have been next to. Shells screamed down – they had got the range now – and we both ducked. As shrapnel whirred overhead someone shouted 'Stretcher-bearer! Stretcher-bearer!' I thanked God I wasn't one. The air grew thick with cordite. Then a howling roar. Sick with fear I braced myself against the ground. It shook as though hit by a gigantic hammer. There was no explosion. Taking a quick look outside the ditch I saw that the shell had landed a foot from my head, leaving a hole just like a rabbit's.

'The bastards are using duds!' I said excitedly.

'No, they're not,' said Baker. 'They're mixing H.E. with armour-piercing jobs. Trying to knock out the trucks.'

My excitement went very flat.

'What do you reckon they are, Titch?' said Phillips, who was on the other side of Baker – '88s?'

'No – 105s. I reckon they'll use up their shit and then they'll fuck off.'

Phillips shook his head.

'I'd like to get my 'ands on the bloke who put us in this flipping field,' he said.

'You're always ticking, that's your trouble,' said Baker, looking more the happy warrior than ever. 'Well, Alec, you'll 'ave something to write 'ome about now. And just think how we'll enjoy talking about it when the war's over.'

'If we're still 'ere,' said Phillips darkly.

Baker accepted the shelling as a matter of course. He kept up a running commentary on its technical side, and he might have been describing a football match. I blessed him for it.

For the next hour the medical orderlies (stretcher-bearers) had a steady trade. The 'grapevine' – primed by Humphreys, who was Company runner – reported two dead and eight wounded. The enemy had concentrated on the trucks, or so Baker thought. Otherwise they must have hit the ditch. When the Battalion M.O. arrived in an ambulance a rifleman from my section went to have a piece of shrapnel removed from his finger. Whilst the operation was in progress the ambulance received a direct hit. The M.O. was killed outright, and the rifleman severely wounded in the back.

I felt surprisingly buoyant, almost exhilarated. During a lull in the shelling Baker lit a cigarette and I opened up a *Times Literary Supplement*. The first thing I saw was the headline: 'The war in Italy: an infantry officer's impression.' I showed it to Baker.

'You'll 'ave some yourself now,' he said.

The shelling slowly petered out. When it stopped altogether we got word to leave the ditch. Officers and N.C.O.s left smartly, the rest of us in slow-time, looking over our shoulders in the direction of the shelling. The ground was riddled with holes – 'rabbit-holes', and the small craters left by high-explosives; I trod delicately, half expecting it to give way. Major Dunkerley and Mr. Simmonds were just ahead of me, alongside a very anxious-looking 'Ginger', his face still partly covered with lather. I heard a familiar whine, and flung myself flat. The shell burst at least a hundred yards away. I felt a fool when I saw both officers still on their feet.

'All right "D" Company! Back to the ditch!' shouted the Company Commander.

I had the luck to team up with Baker again. They were after the ditch now. They got it – fifteen yards from us. Men screamed. Others charged us like cattle. Baker jumped amongst them.

'Don't panic!' he yelled.

They knocked him flat. I tried to get up – to join in the rush not to stop it – but got knocked back into the ditch. I tried again. The same thing happened, only this time I got trampled on as well. The shock sharpened my wits. I stuck out a leg and brought down a pile of men. Jumping up I ran down the ditch. I had caught the panic like a disease. Only when the man behind me stopped running did I flop into the ditch, cursing the men who had knocked me down.

The rifleman behind me crawled up for company. He was in a worse state than I was, understandably so, for his clothes were spattered with blood. I gave him a cigarette. As he smoked he told me how some-one had had their head blown off, and someone else had lost their buttocks. His details were all too graphic. He had to 'get rid of it', but the more he talked the worse I felt. I could have choked him. The only defence I could think of was to have a smoke myself. I put my hand in my trouser pocket to get my pipe. It was gone. I could have cried. Whilst the rifleman talked about the dead I worried about my pipe. My morale had clutched for it like a straw. Its loss sent me to the bottom.

The sound of a low-flying aeroplane pulled me up again. It was a tiny Auster. We waved excitedly. The gunners used Austers to pin-point enemy gun positions. When the plane reached them – they were tucked away in the hills – it almost disappeared in puffs of ack-ack. The pilot circled round as if looking for somewhere to land. A more timely exhibition of courage I can't imagine. When the plane flew back over us the whole Company cheered.

Our guns duly opened up, but the enemy continued to slam the ditch – the part that the Company had abandoned. The direct hits had killed the second-in-command and three riflemen, and our wounded now came to over twenty including Major Dunkerley, Mr. Simmonds, and one of the two remaining platoon officers. The Platoon had escaped lightly. Apart from Mr. Simmonds only three riflemen, all from my section, had been hurt. All this we heard during the four hours or so we were pinned in the ditch. Only when the shelling stopped did we discover why it had been so accurate.

'See that *casa* over there?' said Meadows, pointing to a house about a mile away. 'It was an enemy O.P.*

* Observation Post.

33

They were in touch with a battery of 105s. Major Dunkerley cottoned on to 'em, and one of the tanks went and knocked them out.'

It was only when we had settled ourselves in the three-tonner that O'Connor spoke.

'Have you lost anything, Alec?'

Before I could answer he thrust my pipe into my hands.

'Yerrah. I was the wrong end of the ditch when the bad bit o'shelling started. I was running for me life when I saw a pipe lying on the ground. I'd run another ten yards when I said to myself, that's Alec's pipe, that is, so I ran back and picked it up.'

'Gosh, Paddy,' was all I could say.

Just then Humphreys clambered into the truck. 'We got a cheery sod for a brigadier,' he said. ''e was 'anging about next to where Five Platoon's blokes were buried. Someone 'ad lost 'is mate, and was a bit choked. "Brace up, man!" says the Brigadier. "This is nothing to what you'll get later on." '

We greeted this as Hotspur greeted *his* staff-officer.

The Company moved a mile up the road and harboured in a small field well screened with trees. A red-faced officer in a full-length sheepskin coat waved us in.

'That's Major Henderson,' said O'Connor. 'He's come to take over the Company.'

Five minutes later O'Connor 'scooped' the cooks.

'They found out who put us in the field!' he yelled.

'Who, Paddy!'

He made us wait for it.

'The *Intelligence* officer!'

We howled for his blood.

34

'Intelligence officers?' said Phillips. 'I shit 'em.'

I went to bed feeling curiously happy. The burr of batteries being charged and the distant rumble of guns did nothing to spoil the peacefulness of the night. As I looked at the stars I felt that this time I did have an answer. Number 14407094 was alive and kicking, and had learnt quite a bit.

I was woken up by Swallow shouting 'Wakey! Wakey! Rise and shine!' I pulled the blankets over my head, but he shook them vigorously.

'For Christ's sake,' I murmured.

Rifleman Sullivan, a rookie who had come from another section as a reinforcement, was more explicit.

'Where do you think you are?' he shouted. 'Still in the bleeding barrack-room?'

'Any more of that and you're on a charge!' snapped Swallow.

Soon after we left harbour it rained heavily. It was the first time we had seen any since we landed and we sang like blackbirds:

> 'I don't toil all day
>   Simply because I'm not made that way,
> Some people work for love,
>   They say it's all sunshine and joy
> But if I can't have sunshine
>   Without any work
> I'd sooner stay out in the rain!'

As soon as the rain stopped the sun came out. Everything was sparklingly fresh. Humphreys and Page responded by giving a virtuoso performance of 'Cowboys and Indians'. Humphreys had just uttered

35

a final 'Boom!' when there was a real explosion. Humphreys's face was a picture.

'De-bus, lads,' said Meadows. 'Some Teds up the hill. The mortars are dealing with them. We're standing by, just in case.'

'Those what looks for trouble gets it,' said Gibson, as we climbed out of the truck. 'They weren't causing us any trouble. Why can't we leave them alone?'

'You're a fine soldier, you are!' jeered Baker.

'There they are!' someone shouted.

Through some trees we could see the top half of the hill, and near the summit a vehicle moving along a track. It looked like a Dinky toy, but there was nothing toylike about the mortar-bombs bursting round it. One bomb scored a direct hit.

'That got the bastards!' said Sullivan with relish.

Black dots began running down the hillside. The mortars followed them relentlessly.

'Fuck their luck!' said Gibson.

I seconded that.

The trees prevented us seeing any more of the 'stonk', and the Platoon split up into sections. Swallow's settled down in some long grass near the road.

'Bit soppy pasting a few blokes like that,' said Gibson, removing his steel helmet. The rest of us followed his example. I put mine under my head, soft side up, and used it as a pillow.

Baker fell upon us with a roar.

'Get those bloody steel helmets on!' he yelled. 'You're under observation! You might be under fire any minute! You want to control your section better than this, Corporal Swallow!'

The N.C.O.s glared at one another.

36

'I can look after my section without your help!' said Swallow.

'Let's see you do it then,' said Baker, and left as suddenly as he'd arrived.

Five minutes later Meadows ordered us to withdraw to the road. The mortars were still firing. As we stepped on the road we heard the roar of Bren carriers.

Mr. Lane was in the leading vehicle. We hailed him excitedly. He waved back, then his carrier swung up a side turning. We had hardly had time to remark on his arrival when a white-faced mortarman rushed out of the lane.

'Mr. Lane's dead!' he gasped.

The Platoon stood very still.

'He's dead?' said O'Connor at last, his voice sharp with disbelief.

'Carrier overturned – crushed 'im. The signaller's 'ad it, too. Young "Knocker" White was driving. 'e went into a skid—'

The mortarman's voice cracked. Meadows stepped forward, and put an arm round him.

'Easy, lad, easy,' he said.

'What happened to Knocker?' someone asked.

'Thrown clear. When 'e saw what 'ad 'appened he near went off his nut. Started blubbing, then scarpered. Two of the lads are trying to find 'im.'

The Platoon still hadn't moved. They looked like figures carved in stone.

'Well, lads,' said Meadows. 'Let's go and look after Mr. Lane.'

The carrier had skidded off the track twenty yards in from the road. The head and shoulders of Mr. Lane stuck out from underneath the carrier. The

37

impact had crushed his chest. It had been a quick death. The head of the wireless operator protruded from the other side. His face was blue with suffocation. There was no hope of moving the bodies by ourselves, and Meadows got hold of two more carriers. After some complicated work with tow-ropes they were successful. Meadows then asked for volunteers to carry the bodies. Most of the Platoon moved forward. I was one of the 'jibbers'. The thought of touching dead bodies revolted me. Cooper felt the same way. 'It would make me throw up,' he said.

The bodies were buried in a small clearing. I helped dig the graves, and the physical exertion helped me forget why I was digging them. It's surprising how deep six feet is. Then the regimental padre arrived to read the burial service. Once again the Platoon was divided, only this time more men stayed behind than went. It didn't need much to make the lot of us cry like children. We hung about the truck, finding comfort in our common grief.

As the service ended and the graves were filled in a peasant woman walked up the road carrying a large pot on her head. She passed through us as if we didn't exist. I envied her.

When it was all over the Platoon climbed on board the truck, and Meadows went off on a carrier for orders. When he came back he was smiling. It was a false smile, and we knew it.

'Those weren't Teds up the hill,' he said. 'They were Eyeties. Partisans.'

No one said anything. We stared at Meadows till he could no longer take it. When he had gone I stared at nothing. I was no longer depressed. I wanted to kill. I wanted to kill whoever was responsible for the waste of such a life. Only when I tried to pin the blame did I realize how absurd this was. I might as well try and kill the war.

The truck moved off. No one spoke. The silence became unbearable.

'Poor old Eyeties!' said Gibson nervously. 'If we'd been around when they were getting stonked we'd have learnt some good swear-words.'

It was a brave effort, but it didn't work. We were sick with depression. Until Humphreys burst out singing:

'I don't toil all day,
Simply because I'm not made that way!'

The rest of us joined in, shakily at first, but soon the truck was a blaze of song, and we got rid of it that way.

4
CANTALUPO

By nightfall we were back with the Division. The 'grapevine' insisted Rome had fallen, but by the early hours of the morning our speed had dropped to a walking pace. I sat on the tailboard enjoying myself. I had chosen the tailboard, hard on the bottom, because it was the coolest place in the truck, and, as luck would have it, the night-air was drenched with the scent of wild flowers. I felt quite drunk on it.

Suddenly the smell changed. I got a lung-full of decay. Its virulence turned the night. When it reached a pitch that made me want to vomit the convoy stopped. The smell seeped into the truck. I jumped into the road. Here, at least, the polluted air had no funnel.

Keeping to the crown of the road – the dead would be in the ditches – I walked along like one who knows

> ' . . a frightful fiend
> Doth close behind him tread,'

dreading what I might see, yet needing to see it. The unseen dead stuck in my throat. Two bodies puffed up like Michelin men broke the spell. I shot away from them, up a lane. On a barbed-wire fence hung a vest. Someone had arranged the sleeves in the shape of a cross. The trunk was all bloody and full of holes. The scarecrow, I thought. The Christ. What had the author intended? To shock? To show man's inhumanity to man? To mock God? The lot perhaps.

In the ditch below the vest lay German and American steel helmets, rifles, ammunition, empty tins marked ' "K" Ration'. And something that looked like a white brick. I probed it with my boot. Envelopes spilled over the ditch. I picked some up, amazed how such a neat pile had survived the battle. They were sealed, and addressed in German. Their poignancy struck me like a blow. Who would post the letters of the dead? For God knows how many bodies, buried and unburied, were at hand. I looked up at the vest. A breeze ruffled the trunk, and made a mockery of life. I remembered how I wanted souvenirs. Turning back to the letters I slipped three of them into my wallet. Although there seemed little chance of getting them to Germany one could never tell.

I found Baker bending over the corpses.

'Coming to 'elp me look for a watch?'

My face must have given me away. Baker chuckled.

'Nothing wrong with the dead 'uns,' he said. 'It's the live 'uns you want to worry about. They do pong a bit though.'

After trying unsuccessfully to move one of the bodies he straightened up.

In spite of myself I had to have a closer look. The bloated flesh – the after-effects of rain and sun – was pale green, the same colour as their uniform. There was no telling to which army they belonged.

The sound of a vehicle made us look up. A Jeep

bounced down the lane, then skidded to a halt. One of its occupants stood up.

'Those goddam stiffs still here!' he said.

'Whose are they?' I asked.

'Frog. He's a dirty sonofabitch. Never buries his dead.'

'What's 'appening in front?' asked Baker.

'Our boys are in Rome. I guess we better go find 'em.'

The Jeep shot along the stationary convoy, and disappeared into the night. It was my first encounter with Americans. Their way of going about things was just what I'd expected.

As if galvanized by the Jeep the convoy came to life. As dawn broke we passed the outskirts of a city. It was Rome.

The Company harboured in a vineyard a few miles outside. No one was allowed in, but most of us were more interested in washing and eating than sight-seeing. I was in the middle of shaving when O'Connor nudged me.

'Look at ole Cokey!' he said.

Coke was stripped to the waist, and washing as if his life depended on it. Whatever else Coke might have been he was certainly clean. Giving me a wink O'Connor sidled up to him.

'Oh, Cokey!' he said with a wicked grin. 'You've got a lovely bit o' skin, the best in the Platoon.'

Coke growled and went on washing his face. O'Connor drew his finger down Coke's back. Coke swung round.

'Fuck off!' he said.

O'Connor gave ground.

'If you was a woman, Cokey, what wouldn't I do with you!' he said.

The whole Platoon watching O'Connor crept forward again, and touched Coke on the spine. Coke leapt in the air. Grabbing a naked bayonet he rushed at O'Connor.

'I'll kill you, you Irish bomb-slinger!' he yelled.

O'Connor dived behind the three-tonner, Coke in hot pursuit. They went right round the truck – once, twice, three times, O'Connor laughing, Coke brandishing the bayonet, the rest of us yelling with laughter. Then Baker stepped forward and wrenched the bayonet away.

'Save it for the Germans,' he said.

O'Connor and I went off to forage for food for the section (we were doing our own cooking for the time being). Not far from the harbour I found an allotment rich in carrots, onions, and new potatoes; feeling rather like Peter Rabbit in Mr. MacGregor's garden I took off my beret and filled it up. On the way back to the harbour we spotted some gunners moving into the far end of our vineyard.

'They're Yanks,' said O'Connor happily. 'They'll be good for some fags.'

We hadn't had a N.A.A.F.I. issue since Capua, and I approached the Americans with a mixture of hope and diffidence. I preferred pinching vegetables to cadging tobacco. The Yank I chose must have been all of six foot five.

'I was wondering if you had any tobacco to spare. We've run out,' I said self-consciously.

'Sure!' said the Yank.

Dipping into his haversack he produced four

43

quarter-pound packets of tobacco, and a pile of sweets and chocolate. Such profusion staggered me.

'Can I pay for them?' I said.

'Naw. We've a stack.'

'Are you – are you short of anything?'

It seemed a silly question.

'Waal,' he drawled. 'We could do with some chow. We ain't seen none for two whole days.'

I ran back to the harbour, thinking that our respective quarter-masters should get together. It was simple enough to rustle up some spare tins of stew but I wanted to give my Yank something personal to go with them. Digging out my kit-bag – officially it was at Taranto, but I had given in a spare one – I rummaged around until I reached my books. These included *The Oxford Book of English Verse*, *All Trivia* by Logan Pearsall Smith, a commonplace book with my favourite poems at one end and my own at the other, a first edition of E. V. Lucas's *The Open Road*, Lear's *Nonsense Songs*, a 'collected works' of Shakespeare, and two pocket editions of *Macbeth*. One of them would be just the thing.

Walking back to the Yank I presented him with the stew, then the *Macbeth*, murmuring something about England and souvenirs. Holding the tins in one hand, and *Macbeth* in the other, he looked at them as if they'd come from outer space.

'"*Mac-beth*",' he read out loud, his forehead puckered in a frown. 'By Will-yum—' He paused for concentration. 'By Will-yum Shak-Shak-es-peare?'

He looked at me for guidance.

'He's a – he's an old English author,' I said desperately. Anything to stop laughing out loud.

44

'What part of America do you come from?'

'South Carolina. And I sure wish I was there now,' said the Yank.

I ran back to the harbour hooting with laughter.

The section was enjoying an excellent stew with pancakes to follow, when the cooks' wireless blazed through the vineyard.

'The Second Front's begun!' someone shouted.

The whole Company ran over to the cooks' wagon. An excited B.B.C. correspondent was giving an 'on the spot' description of strafing. In the background we could hear guns, aeroplanes, and bombs. The American battery opened up from their end of the vineyard. As they fired salvo after salvo we all joined arms and careered through the vineyard laughing, shouting and cheering.

An hour later we left harbour. The speed of the convoy – at times we touched 40 m.p.h. – sharpened the scent of victory. The Platoon's three-tonner was *en fête*. An unmistakable 'crr-runch! crr-runch, crr-runch!' of bursting mortar-bombs – it sounded like someone dropping a dinner service – soon changed that. We presumed the enemy were mortaring a unit in front of us. In fact they were putting down defensive fire round a hill-top – which the Company was to stand by to attack. We were to go in riding on the back of Sherman tanks. A few days previously a Guards' company had attacked a hill in similar style. It had cost them ninety per cent casualties. The Platoon's fury broke over Baker. How stupid could the 'brass' get? Hadn't they learnt their lesson – that men on top of tanks were sitting ducks? Baker stood there helplessly, caught between us and the yells

45

from the Platoon behind 'Agitators' ran round fanning the flames.

'Let the "brass" sit on the tanks!' they yelled.

It was the 'round-robin' all over again, only this time the Company meant business. Angry men can be led. So can frightened ones. But men who are both are beyond control. No wonder Major Henderson looked worried.

The men stood round their vehicles like pickets in a strike. Waiting for orders. They were a long time coming.

'It's off!' someone shouted.

A burst of cheering preceded the details. The attack would go in the following day – on foot. The Platoon purred. The Company's little flutter had had results. 'Theirs not to reason why,' is sometimes best forgotten.

The Company harboured in a vineyard. We put up bivouacs for shade. A sudden cloudburst made them doubly useful. I lay in my blankets, listening to the rain, smugly sure that half a spare bivouac I had fixed in the roof would keep it out. Then I felt something cold in my back. I had forgotten to dig any trenches round the tent, and the rain had come *that* way. It was too late to do anything. My blankets were soaked. Looking out of the bivouac I saw O'Connor crawling underneath the three-tonner. With ground-sheet and driest blanket in hand I ran through the mud – the ground had been rock-hard ten minutes earlier – and joined him. Then Swallow squelched over.

'Who gave you permission to leave the section's area?' he asked me, ignoring O'Connor. 'Get back at once!'

Something blew up inside me. I told Swallow exactly what he could do with himself and his orders. The words flowed like water from a tap. I had no idea I could do it. Nor had Swallow. He turned white, and walked away without saying a word. O'Connor was in fits of laughter.

'You told him!' he said. 'You told him!'

My stomach felt full of red-hot needles. I had taken almost as much out of myself as I had out of Swallow.

One by one the Platoon abandoned their bivouacs for the three-tonner. The latecomers, who included Swallow, had to sit inside, under a leaky tarpaulin. O'Connor's blankets were dry, and we made a double bed that saw us through the night most comfortably. In the morning it was still pouring. The vineyard had turned into a bog. To shouts of 'Come to Sunny Italy!' we slopped over to breakfast. Our hopes that the rain would cause the attack to be abandoned came to nothing. The attack was to go in at eleven o'clock. Swallow avoided my eye as he briefed the section. I found this most satisfying.

As the drivers revved-up O'Connor took a long look at the mud.

'They'll have a bit of trouble getting the vehicles out of *this*,' he said.

We boarded the trucks, engines roared, and back wheels spun like tops. We got out of the trucks. The drivers tried without us. The back wheels sank deeper into the mud. Only the fifteen-hundredweights could get clear of it. Major Henderson wirelessed for the carriers to pull us out – and was told that they were stuck, too. They were waiting for the tanks to pull

47

them out. The whole Brigade was bogged down.

This delighted us. A Brigade put out of action by rain. Who would have believed it? Or who, for that matter, would have guessed Major Henderson's next move. The first we knew of it was seeing him walking into the harbour accompanied by a farmer and his ox. A bemused Company watched the farmer hitch the ox to one of the three-tonners. At a shout of '*Ojé*!' the ox took the strain, if you could call it a strain. The ox showed no sign of any. He simply pulled, and the truck followed. Someone said 'Ain't Nature marvellous!', and the phrase echoed round the Company. After coping with three trucks the ox showed signs of tiring. The farmer, primed with a second tin of fifty cigarettes, called up a second ox. Together they finished the job.

The rain had stopped. The sun dried our blankets whilst we were having lunch, and after helping sort out the contents of the colour-sergeant's truck – this had overturned, much to our amusement – we all moved into 'Ox Farm'.

The enemy pulled out during the night. We went after them, into the Sabine hills. Cone-shaped hills fascinate me. The Sabines are exquisitely coned. The villages on top of them merged with the soil like rock. Their bone-white pinnacles were visible for miles. The war had passed the Sabines by – this part of them, at any rate. I was free to marvel at the way the sense of security that had caused the villages to be built on top of the cones had resulted in such fortuitous beauty. Away to the east rose a great mass of snow-capped mountains (they must have been the Abruzzi, which go up to well over nine thousand feet). I stood on the tailboard to get a better view. For once the convoy halted just when I wanted it to.

At our backs was a taped-off cornfield, a sign that it had not been cleared of possible mines, but this didn't prevent Coke disappearing into it with an entrenching tool. When he came back Baker lectured him on when and where to dig a latrine. As if to stress the point two shells landed in the corn. Some hurried orders advised us to dig in on the edge of a neighbouring vineyard.

The enemy only had one gun. The shelling was sporadic and aimless until our own gunners got interested. They were sitting in three Priests – a type of self-propelled gun – thirty yards behind us. As soon as they opened up the enemy concentrated their fire. They fired one shell every five minutes. The Priests replied with three shells every five minutes. We were mixed up in a private war. On the one hand enemy shells, on the other the Priests' guns, which made a noise like the crack of doom. There was no escaping it. Within half an hour I had a splitting headache.

In the lulls between explosions I could hear a lark singing. That made the war seem sillier than ever. I was thinking how man always mucked up nature when I saw two ants on a ledge in my trench. The bigger had the other between its claws, and was dragging it along the ledge. At the corner of the trench the procession halted. The small ant sprang to life and established a stranglehold of its own. Within a few minutes it had dragged its opponent back along the ledge. When it paused for a rest the big ant went into action. He soon made his weight felt. Back went the small ant, like a boxer taking an 'easy' round. The pattern of attack and counter-attack repeated itself, the small ant regaining less and less ground. At the end of one drag it lay motionless. Impressed by its courage I scooped up some dust and let it cascade on to both ants. The victor scurried away. I dug out the small ant, and it was soon as lively as ever. Both ants darted around as if looking for one another, so I arranged a meeting, working it so that the small ant attacked from the rear. They went at it lustily. I decided that a long-range artillery duel had its points.

The enemy suddenly increased his rate of fire. Some near-misses took my mind off the ants. After one explosion I heard Baker yelling at Coke. Looking out of my trench I saw him sitting on Coke's chest, shaking his fist under his nose.

'No one's going to fuck off from my section!' he shouted. 'Get that in your napper!'

Coke slunk back to his trench. Then I noticed one of the Priests was billowing smoke. Two medical orderlies were removing someone on a stretcher.

The remaining Priests began firing flat out. My head was soon throbbing like a motor. If I had known that we were to stay put for another five hours, making eight all told, I think I would have wept. When we did pull out I had just enough nous to notice that the ants were still fighting.

The vehicles had harboured close by. The cooks had a hot meal waiting for us – tinned steak-and-kidney pudding and steamed fruit pudding. It was the best meal we had had since Egypt, and it was well timed.

After we'd eaten Meadows introduced us to a new platoon officer. He was about my own age, and looked pleased with life, too much so considering the news he brought. The Battalion was to attack a village early the following morning. 'A' Company would be on our left, 'C' Company in support. The strength of the enemy was not known. The Guards were dealing with any intermediate opposition. Greatcoats and steel helmets were to be left behind; Bren magazines were to be carried in ordinary (breast) pouches. The village, which was called Cantalupo, was fifteen miles away. We were to travel the first three miles by truck, Four Platoon leading. The Company would leave harbour at 3 a.m.

It was already ten o'clock. The Company bedded down. I was falling asleep when guns opened up from behind the harbour. It was a pepped-up Divisional 'stonk' – two hundred-odd guns. And they were only that many yards away from us. Soon my head was throbbing as badly as ever. I sat up in bed and let the world know about it. Others joined me. We had a brief little barrage of our own.

Sleep was out of the question. Moodily I watched a fringe of trees lit up by gun-flash. The silhouettes were remarkably beautiful.

The barrage ended at 2.30 a.m. As the Platoon assembled by the three-tonner a very subdued Baker reported that Coke and Cooper were missing.

'We can do without Coke,' said Meadows quietly.

I boarded the truck worrying about Cooper. He had been blown up in the Desert; I hated to think of him being court-martialled.

We caught up with the Guards towards dawn. No,

51

they hadn't seen any Germans, one of them said, but they'd lost some men in the barrage. He nodded towards a stretcher. A leg stuck out from under a blanket. Everything about it was just so; the trouser had a knife-edge crease, the gaiter was freshly blancoed, the boot polished. You could see it mounting guard all by itself.

A mile farther on we passed through a Guards' outpost. From now on we were by ourselves. Every square yard of ground had its crater. I couldn't imagine anything living through such a barrage. But an unmistakably German trench, six feet deep and looking as if it had been dug by a machine, was surrounded by half-finished tins of food.

Although we were only a mile or two from Cantalupo we still couldn't see it – there were too many small hills in the way. To avoid these our officers led us on to a dried-up river-bed. We soon halted.

'Teller* mines,' said Gibson. 'Pass it back.'

When I turned round I saw that the rifleman behind me, a newcomer to the Platoon, was standing right on top of one. He was looking at the sky with a vacant expression peculiarly his own.

'Don't look now, Fletcher,' I whispered. 'But you're standing on a mine.'

Fletcher looked down. It took a second or two to sink in. His eyes bulged with shock, and I grabbed him.

'It's all right,' I said. 'It won't hurt you. It's an anti-tank mine.'

The Platoon had just got moving again when there

---

* Teller mines were designed to blow up vehicles, particularly tanks. They would only explode on contact of two thousand pounds or over. This was an article of faith of Battle training.

was a shattering explosion. We went to ground like rabbits. A column of black smoke rose some three hundred yards behind us.

'It's all right, lads,' said Meadows. 'It's the sappers. Blowing up Tellers.'

A rather shamefaced Platoon got to their feet. Leaving the river-bed we re-joined the road. Cantalupo appeared round a bend. It was very close, half a mile away allowing for dead ground, its hill as conical as you could get.

'Fix swords!' said our officer.

We fixed bayonets ('sword' was a regimental term).

'We shall advance to the right of the hedgerow,' said the officer. 'Corporal Swallow, I want you to send out two leading scouts.'

Swallow picked Gibson and myself. We approached the job in different ways. I was proud, excited, and sniffing for Germans. Gibson knew better. 'Don't go so fast!' he kept saying. As we dipped into a straggling orchard the village disappeared. Towards the bottom of the orchard I spotted a farm. At the same moment Gibson saw something the other side of the road.

'There's a *casa* over there!' he said. 'Let's 'ave a butcher's!'

'What about the farm?' I said. 'We're supposed to keep to this side of the road, aren't we?'

'Never mind the farm – you do as I say!'

That did it.

'I'm going to look at the farm,' I said firmly.

Chattering with rage Gibson crossed the road by himself. His exit increased my confidence. For once I and my rifle seemed as one. I was ready for any number of Germans. I bore down on the farm like a tank.

But the buildings were deserted. Disappointed, I stalked towards the hedge bordering the orchard. The village rose in front of me. In the nearest house, only fifty yards away, I saw someone silhouetted against an open window. I couldn't miss him. But at once I realized that the figure was breaking the golden rule of defending a house: never show yourself at the window. Surely no German would do that. Could it be a civilian? I didn't want to shoot some old woman. But why should a civilian stand around like a film gangster? Remembering something about drawing the enemy's fire I very slowly telescoped my head above the hedge. Nothing happened. I pulled it down again. I was wondering whether to report back to the section when I caught sight of 'A' Company's leading scout crawling past a gap in the hedgerow on the far side of the road. I attracted his attention.

'Watch out for that window!' I whispered. 'There may be a sniper!'

He nodded, then wriggled out of sight. A section of men followed him. As I watched the window someone fired a shot from it. A Bren spattered the window sill. Before I could open up myself the orchard was swept by automatic fire.

I dropped on my stomach. Something like eight machine-guns or sub-machine-guns were firing at once. The bullets sprinkled me with leaves. For a few moments I was paralysed with fear. Then, belly to the ground, I slithered back to look for the section. They were lying in a hollow. Before I could say anything Swallow and Gibson were on to me.

'Why didn't you obey orders!' they shouted. 'We thought you was killed! Silly little bastard!'

I tried to explain but they wouldn't listen. When O'Connor weighed in with a word or two of gentle reprimand I gave up. What to me had been a good bit of scouting had resulted in a bollocking. I sat and sulked.

The shooting had stopped. Presently our signaller got in touch with 'A' Company. On the strength of what he heard our officer marched the Platoon up the road. We were in full view of the village yet everything remained mysteriously quiet. If 'A' Company had not been ahead of us I would have suspected a trap. As it was I had some satisfaction in pointing out the sniper's window; the woodwork was well splintered. 'A' Company were resting fifty yards farther up the road. I asked some of their leading Platoon if they had found anyone inside. No, they said; only empty cartridge-cases.

On the threshold of the village we encountered a dead German. A shell had taken off his leg at the hip. He lay in the middle of the road, his staring, agonized eyes drawing ours like a magnet. We walked past him as if our legs were made of glass.

The village had been bombed as well as shelled. As we picked our way through the ruins we ran into some Italians.

'*Partigiani*!' they shouted.

Whilst our officer questioned them in Italian I began to wonder. The partisans were all carrying sub-machine-guns.

'These chaps say the Germans pulled out two hours ago,' said the officer.

That settled it.

'You or your chums shot us up,' I thought.

55

A relaxed Platoon pushed on through the village. It was a big one, about half a mile across. On the far side we found a car park containing nine German half-tracks. They were undamaged. Cock-a-hoop with such booty we roared out insults at the late owners. Humphreys, who was again acting as runner, delivered a message to our officer and joined us.

'Five Platoon found a girl lying in a cellar with 'er throat cut,' he said. 'She 'adn't got a stitch on. The partisans say she's English.'

This was sensational if you like. But before we could comment our officer called the Platoon together, and led us into the grounds of a russet-coloured mansion. To our dismay we marched straight past it on to a sloping lawn, and from there to a kitchen garden.

'What price Company H.Q. in the 'ouse?' said Phillips.

There were no offers. A very bad-tempered Platoon began digging in amongst the cabbages. At least the ground was soft, and I soon scooped out a serviceable trench. I was trying it for depth when Swallow and the officer came round the positions. The officer stopped at mine.

'Corporal,' he said. 'This trench is facing the wrong way.'

'Yessir!' said Swallow. 'You better begin digging another one, Bowlby.'

'I'm not digging another bastard!' I exclaimed furiously.

Swallow and the officer looked a bit shaken.

'Excuse me, sir,' said O'Connor from the flank. 'There's nothing wrong with that trench. I was on the

Desert three years and I never saw a slit-trench facing the wrong way.'

The officer blushed.

'Oh,' he said. 'I see.'

He and Swallow retreated in disorder.

'A slit-trench facing the wrong way!' said O'Connor. 'I never *heard* of such a thing!'

We were discussing Swallow and the officer when we heard a rumble of guns. The whine of approaching shells set us scuttling into our trenches. They burst on the lawn. The next lot smacked into the façade of the house. Some vines covered us from enemy observation and we were just far enough away from the shelling – we were a hundred yards from the house – to be able to watch it. There's a custard-pie element about shells going through windows. When one went straight through the front door we shook with laughter.

Then we heard another noise. It sounded as if the Germans were cranking up an enormous tin-lizzie. The rattle changed to a moan. The moan grew louder. We ducked into our trenches. I had time to notice the exact growth of my fear. It began in the calves, welled up through the loins and stomach, and finally struck home at the throat. As the moan changed to a deafening roar I think I screamed. A series of explosions shook the ground. Part of my parapet fell in. I let it lie on me. Bathed in sweat from head to toe I stared at the holes my fingers had clawed in the clay. O'Connor looked down at me.

'They're "moaning minnies",' he said with a wry grin. 'They sound a lot worse than they are.'

That was something. I had heard quite a bit about

'minnies'. They were six-barrelled mortars that fired six bombs at once. They were deliberately designed to make a demoralizing noise. As far as I was concerned they were an unqualified success. They made any other fear I had encountered seem small beer.

Another rattle sent me to the bottom of my trench. This time the bombs moaned their way over to the other side of the village, where 'A' Company were digging in. The next lot was for us. I felt blown to bits long before they landed.

The enemy alternated between us and 'A' Company with Teutonic rigidity. Although our own guns were probing for the 'minnie' the enemy had stopped shelling. We took to sitting on the side of our trenches when it was 'A' Company's turn for stonking. Once we were all listening to a batch heading their way when the moan crescendoed hideously. The bombs landed before we could move. I saw one burst on top of Meadows's 'trench' – he had scooped a hole in a bank. He emerged white-faced but unhurt. No one had been touched. O'Connor's summing-up of the 'minnie' seemed justified. But I revised my ideas about rigidity.

The enemy gunners opened up again, but they were after our guns. Both sides gave all they'd got. For ten minutes we couldn't hear ourselves speak. When the barrages lifted we argued about how many shells the enemy had fired. Estimates varied between six and eight hundred. Then it began raining. We grumbled at it, loudly.

'A' Company had been caught badly by the 'minnie', and had suffered twenty-odd casualties, including their commander. They had taken six prisoners.

We withdrew at dusk. The trucks were waiting for us on the far side of the village, and took us to harbour.

The Company slept on till a 10 a.m. breakfast. As we were eating Coke and Cooper, who had given themselves up as soon as we'd left for Cantalupo, returned from Battalion H.Q. They had been let off with a warning, along with some other part-time deserters. Coke looked so shamefaced that even Baker let him alone. He came over later to talk.

'I wrote 'ome and told me girl I'm no good,' he said. 'Told 'er I was yellow.'

This touched me.

'You'll be all right, Cokey,' I said, wishing I could sound more convincing. It was different with Cooper.

'I got a bubble on,' he said. 'So I said to myself "Sammy, me lad, you've 'ad this trip".'

When the Platoon had checked their equipment the section-commanders came round making lists of deficiencies. Officially this only covered anything lost or damaged in action. In fact it gave us an opportunity to get something for nothing and we made the most of it. Half of the Platoon put in for emergency rations and khaki-drill trousers. We had discovered that trousers fetched a higher price from the farmers than anything else. The number of pairs listed as 'Lost in Battle' must have run into tens of thousands. But they certainly caused more goodwill than Allied propaganda leaflets written *in English*, telling the Italian peasants 'What Liberation means to *you*.'

In the afternoon a mobile-unit turned up. We enjoyed a hot shower, along with a change of shirts and underwear. Mr. Simmonds arrived with it and took over the Platoon. He told us that the enemy were in full retreat on both fronts, and that we were to join in the advance at dawn.

5
CUCKOOS AT PERUGIA

Three times in the next ten days the Company was briefed for an attack. Each time the Indians got there before us. We loved them for it. All the fun of the chase – with someone else doing the catching. The Battalion's carriers did bump the enemy. On one occasion an 88 knocked out three running before the fourth shot the gun-crew to bits.

Four Platoon surveyed the advance from the back of the three-tonner. Hundreds of bombers flying north excited us as much as they must have depressed the Germans. The sun shone, the country-side was lovely, and cherries were ripe. Once I spent two hours up a tree eating the fruit, for thanks to German bridge-blowing (the sappers worked a twenty-four-hour-day putting up Baileys – without these there wouldn't have been any advance) we harboured every night. If there's a better way of going to war I haven't heard of it.

O'Connor and I bedded down well away from the rest of the section, avoiding the Swallow 'Rise and shine', and only got up when the queue for breakfast had dwindled. Sometimes I preferred an extra lie-in to breakfast. Once I overdid it. The Company drove out of harbour with me still in bed. The Platoon had the treat of watching me run after the truck, throwing my blankets into it as I went.

Fruit-eating caused epidemics of 'gippy-tummy'. Once five of us squatted down together. I was surprised by how homely an affair this was.

On June 18* the Company harboured earlier than usual. We were at twelve hours' notice to move. The first thing I did was sort out my kit-bag. Apart from my books and spare clothing it contained a prized pair of crêpe-soled 'Desert boots', half a German parachute, a folding mirror, fifty feet of rope, a coil of wire, six cigarette lighters, spare pipes, sweets and tobacco.

'Up the Caledonian Market!' cried Humphreys, and grabbed my Desert boots.

''ere, Gibson!' he shouted. 'Sell you Alec's Desert boots for ten fags!'

'Done!' said Gibson.

Humphreys tossed them over. Whilst I was retrieving them Page picked up the parachute and gave us a hula-hula.

Humphreys shook his head at me.

'Just wait till they get you on those bullshit parades,' he said.

I told him I'd wait.

The next morning I woke up on my own accord. Everyone else was still asleep but I felt unusually ready to get up. Encouraged by the sun I took a dip in a neighbouring river, which happened to be the Tiber. The associations added to the swim. On my

---

* At the time I had no idea of the date. Reading the official Regimental History has enabled me to pin-point this and any other date mentioned.

return I found Swallow getting out of bed. He was so surprised to see me up and about he called me by my Christian name.

After breakfast I took Fletcher and a newcomer called Booth down to the river.

A bridge had been bombed, and we dived down to explore some underwater craters. Fletcher stayed down so long we began to get worried. Just as we prepared a rescue act he surfaced like a sealion after fish.

'I loss me teef!' he spluttered. 'I loss me teef!'

It was pure Laurel and Hardy (Fletcher resembled Laurel in looks, as well as deeds). When we had stopped laughing Booth and I dived down in search of the teeth. They weren't to be found. When the Platoon heard about it they gave Fletcher a terrible ragging. But as soon as Mr. Simmonds ordered him to report sick, which meant his going down the Line and at least three days' rest, they changed their tune. It was even suggested that Fletcher had 'worked' the whole thing. Another newcomer called Bennett came to the section in his place.

In the afternoon we had a N.A.A.F.I. issue: ninety cigarettes, a bar of chocolate and a bar of soap, per man (we also had a free issue of fifty cigarettes or a tin of tobacco, and a bar of doubtful 'vitamin' chocolate). Tobacco wasn't rationed. Beer was. We had a pint between three of us. The Eighth Army in Italy's war-cry 'One bottle per man per month perhaps' was pretty accurate.

Armed with soap, chocolate, cigarettes and a spare pair of trousers, O'Connor, Cooper and I set off for the nearest farmhouse. The farmer welcomed us like sons. After giving us all the wine we could drink he bought Cooper's trousers and invited us to dinner. By this time my job as interpreter had ceased to be a strain (I understood the gist of simple Italian without being able to speak much more than the 'Three Dov'é's'* – *'Dov'é casa, dov'é vino, dov'é signorina'*). When the farmer's wife let fly a torrent about 'poor soldiers so far away from their homes and mothers' I was able to pass this on. But it was O'Connor's hour. Producing his crucifix he pointed to himself and said *'Cattolico'*.

The old woman shrieked for joy.

'E Cristiano! E proprio Cristiano!'

She was all over O'Connor, to the extent of producing something special from a small bottle. O'Connor grinned smugly.

Over cigarettes the farmer told me that his three sons had been killed in North Africa. When I tried to convey our sympathy he smiled sadly.

'E la guerra,' he said.

His lack of bitterness left me numb with compassion and guilt.

'What's he on about?' asked Cooper curiously.

When I told him the room suddenly grew quiet. The old woman walked into the kitchen. And then, as if to affirm the continuity of things the daughter of the house arrived with her husband and three delightful children. We rearranged ourselves round the table, and Grandma reappeared with platefuls of spaghetti. We lapped it up.

By the time the meal was over we were all friends

---

* 'Dov'é' is Italian for 'Where is'.

for life. Giving our chocolate to the children, our soap and cigarettes to the grown-ups, we rolled back to harbour. As we went we sang the same song over and over again.

> 'Seven long years you fucked my daughter,
> Now you're bound for the pawnee, Sahib!
> May the ship that takes you homeward,
> Sink to the bottom of the pawnee, Sahib!'

Next morning the war caught up with us. The 5th Battalion had occupied a hill three miles beyond Perugia. This had caused the enemy to abandon positions in front of the town – the Guards had had a bad time trying to take them – and withdrew to the hills north-west of the town. The 1st Battalion had followed up with great dash, dislodging the enemy from Monte Malbe, a hill dominating the town. Initially the Battalion's job was to distract the enemy by attacking the hills to the west of Monte Malbe. The attack would go in that night.

The Company moved to a temporary harbour near Perugia. Here we heard that 'our' hills were held by the same Panzer Grenadiers who had chopped up the Guards in front of Perugia. We were digesting this when it began raining. Our morale drooped. It was only a shower and the 'market' soon recovered. Lance-Corporal Newton had taken no chances with his morale. He had filled two water-bottles with wine and was already half-cut. Newton had volunteered to go overseas when only eighteen, and had arrived in Egypt just in time to qualify for the Africa Star. By day he wore it on his shirt; by night he wore it on his pyjamas (he was the only man in the Platoon to wear them, too). The Desert men ragged him mercilessly but Newton stuck to his medal. As we drove towards our start-line he took a swig from one of the bottles.

'Take it easy, Newt,' said Baker anxiously.

'Don't worry, Titch,' said Newton, waving the bottle. 'There's going to be another M.M. in the Platoon tomorrow.'

We were horrified. If we'd been Catholics we would have crossed ourselves.

'Here's to it!' said Newton, and drank deeply.

At some cross-roads we met two carriers from the 1st. After both parties had remarked on the absence of the 5th one of the carrier-men pointed to a red-roofed villa on top of a hill.

'That's our H.Q.,' he said. 'The lads had a time getting there. They were half-way up when the Teds started mortaring. The lads hit the deck. Then "Bombhead"* started on 'em. "Get up!" he shouts, hitting them on the arse with his swagger. "Get up! They'll get you in the guts! Blow your arse to bits! If you get up, they'll only get you in the legs!" He was right, of course. The lads got up, Bombhead blew his flipping horn, and they took the hill as easy as you like.'

As he spoke a mortar-barrage came down on the villa.

'If that's Battalion H.Q.,' I thought, 'what's it like farther on?'

It was dark when we reached the start-line. We were due to move off at midnight. At half past eleven we were ordered to remove all tracer bullets

* The C.O. of the 1st.

from Bren magazines. The three-tonner's tarpaulin had too many chinks in it for us to risk using it and we had to crawl into a fifteen-hundredweight chock-a-block with bedding and mortar-bombs, and sort out the bullets there (by torch-light). The timing of the order infuriated us. I only saw the funny side when I emerged from the fifteen-hundred weight and heard gusts of swearing passing up and down the Company. It sounded like wind in the trees.

This time Four Platoon were at the rear of the Company, along with H.Q. Platoon. The comforting thought that there were two platoons ahead of us was balanced by the speed of the approach march. We must have been marching at well over 4 m.p.h., and after three hours of it we felt the pace more than the leaders. The section had an additional burden – a drum of signal wire. This weighed a good twenty pounds, and was awkward to handle. After I had taken one particular turn with it Gibson refused to take his. Nothing I said had any effect. And as I was the tail-end of the section I had to hang on to it. I could have murdered him.

We were scheduled to reach the hill at dawn. When it broke we were still on the flat. Luckily a ground-mist covered us from the Germans. A machine-gun warned us we were near them. The bullets weren't aimed at us, but their whip-lash crack made me shiver. So that was a Spandau.

Soon afterwards we reached the foot of the hill. The strain of carrying the drum had exhausted me. When Gibson still refused to take it I flung it on the ground.

'What's up?' said Baker.

I told him. Baker picked up the drum himself.

After ten minutes' climbing I took a rest. Looking over my shoulder I gasped with pleasure. Out of the mist-covered valley three hill-tops rose like islands in a white sea. Their beauty held me spellbound. Whilst men from H.Q. Platoon passed me with curious glances I stood staring at the hills, determined to draw them into myself, so that whatever happened at the top of our hill I should have them to remember. Only when the Company Commander drew level with me did I turn away.

Fantasies of mortar-bombs and Spandaus quickly blotted out the hills.

'They'll open up any moment,' I thought.

To my amazement I found the Platoon squatting in a clearing, like boy-scouts about to pitch camp. Baker grinned at me.

'Yeh,' he said, 'we've arrived.'

It took a while for this to sink in. We had reached our objective without the enemy firing a shot. The crest of hill stuck out thirty yards above the clearing. The slope was thick with bushes and trees, but I could see Five and Six Platoon over to the left, nearer the crest.

Whilst Baker took his section off on a recce the rest of the Platoon began digging in. An inch below the top-soil I struck slate. It was rock-hard. Instead of waiting for my turn with a pick I hacked away with my entrenching tool. After twenty minutes the slate was much the same but I was exhausted.

'I can't get any deeper!' I wailed.

'Let's have a go,' said O'Connor, who had a pick. He soon broke the back of the slate.

At this point Mr. Simmonds decided that the hills across the valley, now clear of the mist, were held by the enemy, and that they might have us under observation. My trench happened to be the only one not covered from view.

'You'll have to stop digging,' he told me.

This annoyed me. The hills were a good six miles away, and it seemed unlikely that the enemy would spot one man digging a slit-trench. But there was no arguing with Mr. Simmonds. Grumbling to myself I lay flat and scratched away with my entrenching tool. Then I heard shouts from the bottom of the hill. The section stopped digging.

'Hans!' someone shouted. 'Hans!'

We grinned at one another.

'We foxed 'em!' said O'Connor. 'We foxed 'em!'

Meadows joined us.

'Fair enough, isn't it?' he said, grinning.

'We've worked it!' said O'Connor. 'They've no *idea* we're here!'

'And Titch is back with a prisoner,' said Meadows. 'A Brigade Q.M.'

'Yerrah! A Q.M.!'

This tickled us no end.

'He was riding along on a bicycle. Titch stepped out from behind a hedge. As easy as that.'

'That's one less of the robbing bastards!' said Gibson.

'Yerrah, it's a pity it wasn't ours!'

Apart from Phillips Baker had no one very reliable in his section (later he told us that the Q.M. had been preceded by lorry-loads of infantry; one look at them and Coke had tried to bolt). It was a personal triumph.

Meadows also told us that the tanks were coming

up in case we wanted their support. This completed the unbuttoning mood begun by the wanderers in the valley. Lolling in our trenches like tourists on a cruise we began discussing the finer points of military tactics. O'Connor soon steered the conversation to the Desert.

'You couldn't have a finer place to fight!' he said.

''ere we go!' said Humphreys, who was eaves-dropping.

'I'm telling you! It was a different sort of war. There were no civvies mixed up in it. It was clean. When we took prisoners we treated them fine and they treated us fine. The fighting was different, too. There wasn't any of this hanging around in the enemy's pockets. We had a go at them, or they had a go at us. Then one of us fucked off!'

'You fucked off about five hundred miles without stopping, if I remember rightly,' said Humphreys.

'Yerrah, that was because your army was still blancoing up. You ought to have been with us then, Alec. There were none of these fucking hills – we didn't march, we drove! And when we went on leave we had eighty or ninety pound to spend. You'd have had the time of your life in Alex! All the beer you could drink. And the women! You've never seen such women! I knew a little Greek bint who'd have been just right for you.'

I dropped off to sleep day-dreaming of Alexandria. The sun woke me. I asked Swallow the time. It was eleven o'clock. Unrolling my gas-cape I draped it round the muzzle of my rifle. The result was a passable sunshade. I then finished my tin of bully, and the last of my water.

70

A shot rang out from the top of the hill. I grabbed my rifle. The bushes. They had covered us from the Germans. Did they now cover the Germans from us? The section glanced at one another nervously, then concentrated on the bushes. A few minutes later Meadows crawled over.

'One of Six Platoon saw a Ted,' he said. 'Took a pot-shot. The cat's out of the bag now.'

But everything remained quiet. After ten minutes the section began to relax.

'Perhaps it was one of the Teds at the bottom of the hill,' I said, without much conviction.

'Yerrah, could be.'

We clung to this like a straw.

From somewhere the other side of the hill an 88 opened up, but its shells landed in the valley.

Half an hour went by and still nothing happened. Then the cuckoos began calling. There were two of them. Their homely notes cheered us up no end. O'Connor told a tale of cuckoos in Cork and I weighed in with one of my own. It began to look as if we hadn't been rumbled after all.

Mr. Simmonds had laid on an observation post a little way down the hill, and I went down to relieve Bennett. He was lying under a rock, watching something through binoculars. I soon saw what it was. The 88 behind the hill was shelling a cross-roads. The smoke from the shell-bursts disappeared before the sound reached the hill. The puffs of smoke appeared and vanished like a conjurer's rabbit.

Across the valley I spotted six Shermans. They were trundling along the same road the Company had taken. As they neared the hill the 88 stopped firing.

71

'Why?' I thought.

The tanks parked themselves at the bottom of the hill. They were a most reassuring sight. I crawled back to Swallow and reported. On my way back to the rock I saw the ground round the tanks erupt in mortar-bombs. For a while the tanks performed a sort of mechanical dance, jerking backwards and forwards, in an effort to avoid the bombs. Then they turned tail and headed for the road. I waited for them to re-form. They kept going. When they were out of sight I ran back to the section.

'They've buggered off!' I shouted.

I had to give details before anybody would believe me. The tank-crews came in for a terrible clobbering.

When I returned to the rock the 88 began firing again. This time it was after a house. The first shell landed a hundred yards away, the second fifty, the third twenty-five.

'The next will be bang on,' I thought.

I heard the explosion but I couldn't *see* it. I stared at the house, wondering how on earth I'd missed the burst. Then there were more explosions. Bits of shrapnel flew over the rock. Swallow shouted me back to the section. A piece of shrapnel followed me into my trench. I picked it up and burnt my fingers.

It was a mortar-barrage, as intense as the one I had seen going down on the tanks. Several near-misses kept my head down. Then I heard a mortar firing; the report was distinct. The bomb landed between my trench and the bushes. The mortar fired again. This time the bomb was closer. Was the mortarman after my trench in particular? The idea terrified me. The next bomb blew in half my parapet. I wasn't waiting for any more.

'I'm getting out, Paddy!' I yelled.

'Stay where you are, Alec,' said O'Connor firmly. 'You'll be all right.'

I flopped back in my trench and the bomb I expected never came. Our own guns opened up. The shells screamed over, landing just the other side of the hill.

'Go on, kill them!' I snarled. 'Kill the bastards!'

For the first time in my life I enjoyed the thought of men being blown to bits.

The mortaring stopped as neatly as a curtain-fall. We looked at one another without speaking. The silence worried me as much as the mortaring. Were they going to rush us? They used Spandaus instead. Bullets swept our positions. The crackling made me duck. With an effort I poked my rifle out of the trench and looked out. Lance-Corporal Newton was running up the hill firing his Tommy. A Spandau fired. Newton fell. As he hit the ground a mortar-bomb landed by his legs. Another burst near my trench. I ducked out of sight. Brens opened up on the left. Compared with the Spandaus they sounded like pop-guns. Cries of 'Stretcher-bearer! Stretcher-bearer!' alternated with long bursts of Spandau. I kept ducking up and down.

It stopped as suddenly as before. Our own guns lifted as well. Newton's body had been removed. O'Connor lay in his trench, his face grey with strain.

'I think Newt's had it,' I said.

Then I saw Bennett slumped face downwards in his trench. One eye on the bushes I crawled over to see if he was dead or wounded. He was unconscious

73

but breathing normally.

'My God!' I thought, 'I believe he's asleep!'

I poked him in the ribs; he woke up, and yawned.

'He was asleep!' I said to O'Connor, and then sat in my trench, wondering just what would happen next.

The sun was less fierce now. I sucked at my empty water-bottle, then made a less obvious shade with my gas-cape.

Down in the valley a Spandau opened up. It fired burst after burst. As if in answer there was a burst of cheering. The Spandau fired a ten-second burst. My stomach turned over.

'If blokes can charge a Spandau,' I thought, 'we can stick it up here.'

Bennett was now sitting on the side of his trench, swinging his legs. At that moment I would cheerfully have swopped heads with him.

'There's a tank up there,' he remarked casually.

'It's about bloody time they turned up,' I said, trying to spot it.

'I don't think it's one of ours,' said Bennett.

A gun fired. Its shell screamed through the trees. The whole orchestra started up – big mortars, small mortars, Spandaus, Brens, rifles, grenades. The tank's 88 fired 'cheesecutters'. Two Spandaus raked the section's position. Our own guns opened up. The whole hill shook with explosions. Then I heard a peculiar 'wurra-wurra!' Small shells smacked into a tree growing out of my trench. I could see the white-hot steel. They were cannon-shells. The tank was using the tree as an aiming post. Hypnotized with fear I watched the tree slowly disintegrate.

'Prepare to withdraw!' shouted Mr. Simmonds.

I pulled on my greatcoat over my equipment.

'Withdraw!'

The Platoon fled. Major Henderson was walking the rest of the Company down the hill. He was looking very thoughtful. He halted us in a clearing half-way down the hill.

'They'll probably try a box-barrage,' he said, 'so we'll stop here.'

The Company sat down and waited. Sure enough a murderous barrage came down at the foot of the hill.

'That was a crafty move!' said Baker. 'See that "Tiger"? Big as a fucking house. Poor old Newt. They don't think 'e'll live. 'e asked for it, though.'

Baker also told me that three out of the four stretcher-bearers had been wounded whilst giving first-aid. No one had been killed outright.

'We ain't done bad,' he added. 'Phillips got three of them with the Bren, and I nabbed a couple. Five Platoon got a stack.'

'All right, "D" Company,' said Major Henderson. 'We'll return to the positions.'

This made me feel cold all over. But Henderson knew his stuff. I climbed the hill wondering if the Germans had occupied our positions. They hadn't. A depleted section – Gibson and Sullivan were helping to carry wounded back to our own lines – dropped into the trenches.

A Bren opened up. The whole show began again. Only this time the noise seemed worse than ever. It hammered my nerves to jelly. I tried to concentrate on the hills rising out of the mist. Noise swept them away. When I heard a rush of feet I lay on my back waiting to be bayoneted. I couldn't even have raised my hands above my head. But the feet passed my trench. Looking out I saw the Platoon running down the hill. Leaping out of my trench I raced after them. I'd gone fifty yards before I realized I had left my rifle behind.

The remnants of the Company were gathered in the clearing. Very conscious of my lack of arms I asked Mr. Simmonds if I should go back for my rifle.

'No, I don't think so,' he said. 'I'll ask the Company Commander.'

Major Henderson had a look at me.

'Yes,' he said. 'I think you should get it.'

Back I went, wishing I had kept quiet. I was soon crawling. Every few yards I stopped to listen. Everything was still. The positions were just as we had left them. I could see my rifle lying on the parapet. As I crept towards it someone spoke. I froze. An answering voice came from the same place – higher up the slope. Wriggling over to the trench I grabbed my rifle, jumped to my feet and raced down the slope. I ran so fast I went head-over-heels – and kept going that way, deliberately, for at least thirty yards. I guessed a tumbling target would be difficult to hit.

When I reached the clearing I found it deserted. It was one of the worst moments of the day. I felt horribly lost. Running on down the hill I spotted a rifleman, near the bottom. When I got there I saw seven or eight more running across a field towards a wooded slope a quarter of a mile away. As I ran after them guns opened up. The shell burst amongst us. As if in a dream I saw the others run on unhurt. They kept running. I threw myself flat at every burst. In spite of this I slowly gained on them. Every moment I expected to be blown to bits. How could one survive shells bursting at one's feet? Yet even then part of me was noticing how red the flames were. Nothing could stop me recording. But my bouncing burned me up physically. As I neared the slope my knees stopped working. I fell in a heap. My greatcoat felt like a leaded shroud. With one last effort I got up and staggered to the slope.

Recovering my breath I crawled up the slope in search of the others. They were standing on a path, O'Connor, Mr. Simmonds, Swallow and Major Henderson amongst them. Some shells crashed into the undergrowth below us. We moved into a ditch above the path. On my left I had a signaller, on my right Mr. Simmonds. Major Henderson was on the extreme left of the group, next to the signaller.

'I think we should clear out now, John, don't you?' he said.

'Wouldn't it be better to wait till it's dark?' suggested Mr. Simmonds.

'One up to you,' I thought.

Major Henderson looked at his watch.

'It's only six now,' he said. 'It won't be dark until nine.'

Whilst they continued the discussion I filled my pipe. As I went to strike a match a Spandau opened fire. From twenty yards farther up the slope. The bullets weren't aimed at us. The shock struck almost as hard. I was petrified. Like a Pompeian sentinel. Pipe in mouth, match in hand, I stared at Mr. Simmonds. He stared back. Unmoved. A mortar fired. It was in the same place as the Spandau, not more than twenty yards farther up the slope. The bomb sailed off towards our own lines. The Germans began talking. One of them shouted. An answering cry came from the foot of the slope. I counted four voices there, one of them a woman's. Could they be Italians? Mr. Simmonds had the same thought. He slowly swivelled round towards the rifleman the other side of him, who spoke fluent German. The rifleman shook his head, and mouthed the word 'German'.

As I glanced at the bushes shielding the ditch, and worked out our chances of leaving it alive, one of the Germans at the top of the slope began singing. It was on the lines of the *Horst Wessel*, and reeked of victory and *Deutschland über Alles*. The singer did it proud. He was a big bugger, by the sound of him. Although very much aware of how easily he could sling us a grenade I couldn't help enjoying the irony. I grinned ruefully at Mr. Simmonds. He looked straight through me.

In the middle of the second verse guns opened up from our own lines. The shells landed on the slope. The Germans shouted at one another. The barrage only lasted a few minutes but it was enough to make them dig in. I thanked God for the gunners. Whilst the Germans were digging we could afford to relax a little, to straighten our legs, and move an arm. When they stopped only snatches of conversation broke the silence. Finally everything was quiet. The slightest rustle could give us away. And there were two hours to go.

As I sat in the ditch I was aware of a *creeping* fear. The longer the silence the worse the fear. I longed for noise, any noise, even the noise on the hill. In lieu of it I began praying, a stream of promises of what I would do if God would let me leave the ditch alive.

'And if I do get out,' I thought, 'I'll desert. Anything's better than this.'

Footsteps began crunching down the slope. They were heading straight for the bush in front of me. I released the safety-catch of my rifle. As I pointed it at the bushes Mr. Simmonds put a finger to his lips. I wondered whether the German would surrender or if I would have to shoot him.

'One shot and we've all had it,' I thought.

I also decided that a Tommy would have been much more useful than a rifle. I made a mental note to get myself one – if we ever got out of the ditch.

The German halted behind the bush.

Had he twigged?

Then I heard a steel belt-buckle being loosened. Other noises followed; it sounded as if the German was having a shit; a rustle of paper confirmed this.

I grinned at Mr. Simmonds. Again he looked straight through me. The German re-buckled himself, and walked back up the slope. The wood began to roar with silence. After more prayers I looked round to see how other people were taking the strain. Mr. Simmonds was as poker-faced as ever. The German-speaking rifleman was bowed down by the weight of an enormous wireless. Behind him O'Connor was clutching a spare Bren barrel and looked ready to conk the first German he saw. When I looked at the signaller I had a shock. He was asleep. This seemed on a par with Bennett. Major Henderson was looking at his watch. As the light faded he mouthed a message warning us that we were moving out in five minutes; we were to leave the ditch in single file, one at a time.

Deciding that our chance of survival would depend more on speed than guile I began shedding my greatcoat. To do this in silence required time, and I had only just managed it when Major Henderson stood up. As I stood up myself Mr. Simmonds dug me in the ribs. I turned round. He pointed at my greatcoat. Cursing him silently I picked it up.

Major Henderson stepped gingerly out of the ditch; the signaller followed. A twig cracked under him. As I moved on to the path I trod on another.

'*Halte*!'

I swung round instinctively. A figure stood silhouetted against the sky. I ran down the slope. The sentry opened fire. As rifle-bullets whistled past the ground gave way under my feet. My greatcoat flew out of my hand.

'Good riddance!' I thought, and then hit the ground like a bomb.

I jumped up quickly, saw that I'd fallen twenty feet – that part of the slope ended in a cliff – then ran after Major Henderson, who was disappearing round the corner of the slope.

The Germans were shouting their heads off.

'That shook the bastards,' I thought.

As the rest of the party joined us two Spandaus opened fire. The bullets were nowhere near us but O'Connor and another rifleman were to come. I was beginning to get worried when O'Connor ran in.

'Ward went down when the Spandau opened up, sir,' he said. 'He's not hurt, but he wouldn't get up.'

For the first time that day Major Henderson didn't

have a ready answer. As he stood there, obviously debating whether we should go back for the rifleman or get clear ourselves, I put my oar in.

'If we don't move out, now, sir, we'll never get out.'

To my surprise Major Henderson nodded, then led us into a cornfield. We were half-way across when a Spandau opened up. Tracer bullets lit up the party – I had a split-second recollection of our removing the Bren tracer – and we ran. The tracer whipped between us as if the Spandau-man had orders to just tickle us up.

'Battle-course gone wrong,' I thought, and then my underpants came down.

I went headlong. Scrambling up I plunged forward in childlike rushes, my pants round my ankles. Again and again I crashed into the corn. Sobbing with rage, my face knocked raw by the stubble, I tried desperately to keep up with the others. As I dropped behind it seemed that the Spandau must get me. He didn't, and I caught the others up behind a hedge. Whilst they rested I pulled up my pants.

The Germans tossed us a couple of mortar-bombs. We moved into the next field. I had no idea where we were but Major Henderson was handling a compass with a professional air. He knew.

On the far side of the field we passed a German lorry. No one challenged. I would have shot them happily if they had.

We kept going until we heard track-vehicles on a road. We headed towards them cautiously. Were they ours?

'Whoa-back!' someone shouted.

I've never heard a sweeter sound.

For some reason Major Henderson led us towards the road via the top of a bank. The slope we had left was bathed in moonlight. It was not all that far away. The party would be sky-lined on the bank. I kept off it, and cursed Major H. I listened for the enemy mortar and heard it fire. I hit the ground a split second after the bombs – one of them landed smack on the bank. The party ran off it, and we all legged it for the road.

The vehicles belonged to the Battalion's mortar-section. They were preparing to lay down a barrage for the 5th, who were attacking on our hills. Major Henderson commandeered one of the vehicles. Five of us piled on it. As we drove off we passed two companies of the 5th. They had the wary, haunted look of men going into a big attack, and I pitied them.

'D' Company were harbouring a few miles away. Meadows met the carrier.

'We thought you'd had it,' he said.

As I gobbled down steak-pie and jam-tart I told him what had happened in the ditch. He told me that all the Platoon were accounted for except Ward.

I took to my blankets and was asleep in no time at all.

6
INTERLUDE

The sun woke me up. At once I knew there was something to be happy about. Then I remembered. I had escaped. I was alive. The joy of this swept through me. I stretched myself like a cat, loving the touch of the blankets, and looked up at an olive-tree shimmering in the sun, and loved that, too. But a jangle of mess-tins broke the mood. Why should anyone be *running* with mess-tins? I sat up, and saw it was Gibson.

"'ere!' he shouted. 'You know that company of the 5th what relieved us! They got wiped out! The Germans charged 'em!'

I had an immediate and overwhelming sense of horror – and guilt. As Gibson gabbled on I saw the attack, and heard the screams. They had been killed instead of us. Had they been killed because of us? Should we have stuck?

'No,' I thought. 'We had our share. It was just bad luck.'

But was it?

At breakfast I heard the details. The enemy had attacked at six-thirty – our signallers had picked up an SOS – without any warning barrage. They had got amongst the 5th before they could call for artillery support. Half the Company were dead, the rest wounded or prisoner.*

'D' Company's casualties were eighteen wounded and two missing. Ward had been picked up – by a reserve company of the 5th – unhurt but suffering from shock. He was on his way to hospital. Newton was already there. With luck he'd pull through.† Gibson told us some yarn about not having heard the order for the Company's first withdrawal, and how he'd shot a German all by himself. The shooting part didn't sound very convincing, but I could understand his not having heard the order. Apparently the second withdrawal had also been 'official'. Major Henderson had ordered each man for himself. I had been too dazed to hear Mr. Simmonds pass this on. The Company had not cut and run, as I had presumed, and this made me feel a bit less guilty about the 5th.

O'Connor added a tailpiece to our experiences in the ditch.

'You know that at my end of it there was a German up a tree?' he said. 'All he had to do was look round. He'd have seen the lot of us. I tell you we don't have to worry any more. If we can get out of that ditch we can get out of anything. You see. And I'll tell you something else. I've climbed my last hill. I'm too old for all this running about.'‡

---

* This was inaccurate. The Company Commander, one platoon officer, and eight riflemen were killed, thirty wounded, and two officers and thirty-three riflemen taken prisoners, a number of them wounded.
† He did, but he was crippled for life.
‡ O'Connor was thirty-three. The average age of the Platoon was about twenty-four.

The Company was moving harbour.

When we arrived at the new one the enemy began shelling it. They couldn't possibly have seen us. It was just luck, the sort to make one wonder. A jumpy Company took shelter in a barn. Once the shelling eased we moved on again.

The convoy stopped outside a villa. Its duck's-egg-green tiles contrasted splendidly with its white-washed walls.

'We're here for a week,' Meadows told us. 'Perhaps longer.'

We cheered like schoolboys.

When we sorted out our equipment we had some surprises.

'Look at that!' shouted Sullivan.

Embedded in his Bren magazine pouch was a lump of shrapnel the size of a golf-ball. Sullivan slipped on the pouches. The shrapnel lay over his heart.

O'Connor gave Gibson the spare Bren barrel.

'I carried it all the way back for you,' he said, proudly.

'Well, it ain't much. I 'ad to leave the Bren be'ind when I took a stretcher,' said Gibson. 'Any'ow, it's duff.'

'Yerrah? Duff?'

'Look at it. Shrapnel.'

O'Connor looked. Then he whirled it round his head, and sent it flying.

'To think I carried the bloody thing all those miles! To think of it!'

After Swallow had taken my deficiencies – a rich haul this time, greatcoat and beret actually lost, trousers and emergency rations 'lost' – I rolled out my blankets to air in the sun. Then I went to have a look round the villa.

'There's a garden on the inside,' someone told me.

Crimson and orange borders spilled over the lawn with the cornucopian profusion of wild flowers. Only a master-gardener could have given Mother Earth her head, and still kept her in bounds, for bounds there were. Each section of the garden harmonized with the other. They had even thought of the light. The flower side was diamond-bright – the sun-drenched walls of the villa saw to that. The lawn side lay in the shade. Sun without cypresses would have been too much.

The sound of bees humming in the flowers mingled with the hiss of a fountain. I walked towards the pool like a man in a trance. The marble rim was hot with the sun. When I sat down I had the spray on my face, the flowers to smell, a warm bottom, and the fountain to listen to. The sound bound everything together. Closing my eyes I let it come inside.

'Lovely, ain't it?'

It was Cooper.

I nodded, too happy to speak. He sat down beside me. O'Connor soon joined us.

'What a place to live, Paddy!'

'Yerrah, it belongs to a bishop. They do themselves well. There was one I knew in County Cork. He liked a drop of Guinness, he did. One day he came along to me . . .'

For once O'Connor's story-telling failed to hold me. The fountain had come right inside. *It* held me.

The Platoon were quartered in a long room with

86

angels painted on the ceilings. After some inevitable comments from Humphreys about how we'd have to behave ourselves with them watching over us we settled down for the night. I was half asleep when I heard a gun fire. The shell landed about a mile away. The gun fired again. This time the burst was much closer. All of us must have had the same thought, but Phillips had to put it into words.

'I reckon they've rumbled us,' he said.

No one answered him. More shells burst round us.

'These slates won't keep much out,' said Phillips.

'Oh, dry up, Phil, will you!' said Humphreys.

Some shrapnel hit the roof.

'I reckon—' began Phillips.

We yelled at him, and someone threw a boot.

'Bomb-'appy lot, ain't you,' said Phillips, cheerfully.

The shelling continued, but there were no direct hits. We decided that a 'Tiger' or S.P. gun had crept round the hills, and was after some local twenty-five-pounders. The intruder left an hour or so before dawn.

On their way back from breakfast half the Platoon washed their mess-tins in the fountain. This appalled me, but I didn't fancy acting as custodian. I just removed the bacon-rind and bread. There wasn't much I could do about the porridge.

At ten o'clock all company N.C.O.s reported to Battalion Headquarters. Meadows and Baker came back looking completely demoralized. For a while they just looked at us. Finally Meadows got it out.

'The C.O.'s called us a lot of gutless swine,' he said.

It was like a blow in the face. For a moment we

were speechless. Then out it came.

''e 'asn't got the guts to come round 'ere and tell us!' (Humphreys, I think.)

'Yerrah, he wants to get up there his bloody self!'

'It was each man for himself, wasn't it?' (Gibson.)

As the storm died down Phillips said 'What about those fucking tank wallahs? They fucked off in a cart-load of armour, and they expect us to stick!'

Meadows shrugged.

'The C.O.'s had a row with the tank C.O.,' he said.

'Bloody good of 'im!' said Gibson.

Meadows waited for us to stop muttering, then went on: 'The R.A.F.'s going to bomb the hill this afternoon.'

'Pity they didn't think of that before, ain't it?' said Humphreys.

Meadows rode that one.

'And you know those cuckoos?' he said. 'They were Teds. Signalling.'

By the time we had got over our surprise the proceedings were over. The C.O.'s outburst had obviously been influenced by the fate of the 5th. But had we been so gutless? Who knew how many men the Company had killed on the hill?

In the late afternoon, when the air was soft and infinitely peaceful, the Battalion padre held a service for the dead. Several hundred men attended, and we stood in line facing the same hills.

'I will lift up mine eyes unto the hills from whence cometh my strength,' read the padre.

I looked at the hill, thinking of the men who had died there, and how close I had come to it myself. But as the padre read on it became more and more

88

difficult to think of the dead as dead. The words of the psalm, the serenity of the hills, the touch of the sun on my face, confused them with the living to such an extent that for a moment I felt sure there was a God.

Next morning Major Dunkerley came back to take over the Company. Meadows told me I was on Company Office.

'He's found out about those emergency rations!' was my immediate reaction.

Then I realized I wasn't the only one who worked that.

'What am I up for?' I asked.

Meadows only grinned.

'I'll tell you,' said Humphreys. 'You're up for a stripe, my lad! Lance-Corporal Bowlby! Cor!'

I grinned back at him.

'You won't catch me taking a stripe!'

The 'office' was in a tent on the far side of the villa. As I walked over I had plenty of time to run over my pursuit of, and retreat from, promotion.

I had volunteered for the Army – I hadn't fancied being called up – and this, plus the fact of my having been to one of the public schools which the regiment preferred its officers from, automatically earmarked me as a potential officer. This upset my platoon sergeant even more than my arms-drill. One bleak November morning he could stand it no longer. The squad was practising gas-drill. I had hidden myself in the back rank but the Sergeant had turned the squad round. When everyone else had replaced their respirators I was still wrestling with the head-piece. The eye of the Sergeant was upon me. Desperately I

rammed home the head-piece. When I buttoned up
the respirator it bulged like a pregnant serpent. The
Sergeant moved in for the kill. Unbuttoning the respirator he replaced it correctly. Then he thrust his
face into mine.

'If you ever get a commission my prick's a bloater!'

A week later I was sent to a War Office Selection
Board. Its highlight was an interview with a psychiatrist. I thought this would be fun. When I entered his
room I had to stop myself giggling. He motioned me
to sit down, and continued to correct papers (we had
all answered a word-association test). After five minutes' silence I no longer found anything funny about
the interview. After ten minutes I felt like screaming.

The psychiatrist suddenly looked up from the
papers. He stared at me until I had to look down.

'You were unhappy at school, are extremely self-
conscious, and find it difficult to concentrate. Correct?'

I nodded dumbly, wondering how on earth he did
it.

'Both your parents are neurotic, aren't they?'

'I – I don't know.'

'H'm. Have you ever had a woman?'

'No.'

'Do you want to?'

'Of course!'

The psychiatrist gave me another long stare. I
ended up looking at the floor.

'What do you like most in life?'

'Poetry, I suppose.'

'Why?'

'Because it's part of my ideals.'

'What ideals?'

'I don't quite know how to explain. I suppose my ideals are what I believe in.'

'What do you believe in?'

'Helping other people. Doing what I feel is right.'

The psychiatrist leant across the table.

'What would your feelings be if you bayoneted a German?'

This was much better.

'I'd feel sorry for him. I don't think he would have caused the war any more than I did.'

The psychiatrist frowned.

'Well, what would you feel if *you* were bayoneted by a German?'

'A great deal of pain.'

'Yes, but *what else*?'

I couldn't think of anything else.

'Nothing.'

The psychiatrist glared at me. I stared back. We looked at each other until I felt dizzy.

'You should avoid going out alone at nights,' he said finally.

I nearly burst out laughing. But he hadn't quite finished.

'And if you don't give up these so-called ideals of yours you'll go mad within eighteen months.'

I was so shaken I couldn't speak. Finally I said: 'But what shall I do?'

'That's up to you.'

When I got out of the room I fainted.

For some weeks afterwards my nerves were all to bits. I lived for letters from a friend who slowly convinced me that the psychiatrist was talking through his hat.

There were three grades of failure at the Selection Board. You either returned in three months, in six months, or not at all. To my surprise I only got three months. In between times came a dinner at a club thick with staff officers. My host was a retired Colonel, my fellow guest a young subaltern from the Rifle's sister regiment – who had got his commission before psychiatrists had their say. He wanted to know what they did. After telling them that I and the psychiatrist were at one in considering that I wasn't ready for a commission, and that I had expected to be failed completely, I described the interview. Colonel and subaltern enjoyed themselves. So did I.

The time came for my second Selection Board. But first I had to satisfy my training C.O. that I was ready for it. I had not enjoyed my three months. My Platoon were all 'rejects' like myself, but unlike me most of them had set their hearts on a commission. They made up for their lack of quality by a most ferocious keenness. Some of them polished the studs of their boots. Others sucked-up. I did not compete. When I was marched into the Battalion Office I just had time to glimpse at least twenty officers lined up behind the C.O. before he blew his top.

'Rifleman Bowlby!' he yelled. 'You're a disgrace to the Regiment! You've run down an officer holding His Majesty's commission! There's no worse crime in the British Army!'

As the C.O. paused for breath I began to realize what it was all about. The psychiatrist.

'And, furthermore,' said the C.O., 'you've attempted to use influence to obtain a commission yourself, something I thought no rifleman capable of!'

'That's not true!' I said.

'Don't argue with me!' said the C.O.

'Keep quiet!' said the R.S.M.

'Even if this incident hadn't happened,' continued the C.O., 'your training record would have disqualified you from attending the Board. I have decided to send you to a service battalion, so as you can find out what real soldiering is like. I shan't mention this incident in your confidential report. You will still be a potential officer. And you will leave as soon as the transfer can be put through.'

I was marched out of the room crying with rage. I didn't give a damn about the Board, but the accusations stuck in my throat. I soon discovered that the Colonel of the Selection Board I had attended had been staying in my Colonel friend's club the same night. For a long time I presumed that someone had given him a highly-coloured account of what I had said at the dinner. It's more likely that my friend had innocently remarked to him on the oddity of the psychiatrist's questions, and asked him if he thought that psychiatrists were really any use in picking officer material.

By one of those glorious freaks of chance that only happen in something like the Army I suddenly no longer existed. My training company appeared to think I had gone off to O.C.T.U. with all the other potential officers – the whole Platoon had passed the Selection Board – and I was free to do exactly as I pleased until someone woke up. Every day for five weeks I caught the first bus into town. I spent the mornings quietly in the lounge of the best hotel. It wasn't safe to be out and about without a pass before

noon and mine were forged anyway. In the afternoon I wandered round the town or went to a film.
One morning I met the C.O. coming round the
chapel which was next to the bus-stop. Before he recognized me his dog went after a cat. I slipped behind
the chapel. Another time I was walking along a path
in some gardens. It was a beautiful spring morning
and although I had no pass of any sort I decided to
risk the Military Police. Half-way across the gardens
I saw two of them standing by the path. I about-
turned and saw four more behind me. Swallowing
hard I turned round again. Two was better than four.
As I approached the red-caps one of them said something to his colleague and stepped forward so I
would have to pass right by him. The doors of the
Glasshouse opened before me.

'It's a lovely morning, isn't it?' said the red-cap
pleasantly.

'Yes, lovely.'

I waited for the bullet.

'All the flowers coming up,' said the red-cap. 'Birds
singing. You wouldn't know there was a war on,
would you?'

I agreed with him. The man was genuine. He just
wanted to show me that all red-caps weren't
bastards.

After five weeks my transfer came through. I went
to a service battalion of the Rifle's sister regiment.
The Platoon I joined was one hundred per cent cockney. After the 'reject' platoon it was like a breath of
fresh air. And for the first time in my life I was
accepted for what I was rather than what I ought to
be. I relished the warmth and wit of the cockneys,

and they and the comparative happy-go-lucky atmosphere of a service battalion turned me into quite a competent rifleman. 'Real soldiering' suited me. But then my Company Commander reminded me that I was a potential officer, persuaded me to take a stripe, and in due course packed me off to another Selection Board. I failed completely. In the six months I had been with the Battalion I had felt myself surrounded by the salt of the earth. I imagined I could now enjoy it permanently. But They decided that I must return to my own regiment. I tried to change regiments. This was not allowed. When I realized I would have to go I burst into tears. Back I went to a training depot. Within three months I was on my way overseas. Only when I reached the 3rd Battalion did I begin to realize that life has its own way of arranging things.

My six months as a lance-corporal – I kept the stripe until Egypt – had convinced me that I was better off as a rifleman. Three weeks' fighting had confirmed this. Riflemen lived longer than N.C.O.s. I prepared a suitable rejection story for Major Dunkerley.

He was sitting at a table, Major Henderson standing beside him.

'I hear you gave a good account of yourself up the hill,' said the Company Commander.

What on earth was he talking about?

'That damn rifle,' I thought.

'We were wondering how you felt about taking a stripe.'

'Well, sir, I don't feel I've seen enough action yet. And I think that some of the other men in the Platoon would make better N.C.O.s. than I would.'

'Yes, we thought you might feel like that. We've decided to make you a medical orderly. It's a dangerous and responsible job. Will you accept the post?'

I was so surprised I said 'Yes'. I arrived back with the Platoon in a daze.

'They've made me a stretcher-bearer, Paddy!' I said excitedly.

'Yerrah? That won't suit you, Alec. You haven't got the stomach for it. Besides, you'd have to leave the Platoon.'

The implications of the job suddenly hit me. I would be lost without the Platoon.

'What'll I do?' I said desperately. 'How'll I get out of it?'

'Go and tell Major Dunkerley you've changed your mind. Tell him you'll take it on in an emergency. He's a gentleman, is Dunkerley. He'll understand. Now stop looking worried and sit down.'

It panned out just as O'Connor had said it would.*

That afternoon the Company paid its first visit to Perugia. As we neared the top of the great corkscrew road leading to the upper part of town we passed a regiment of tanks, obviously billeted there. They cut short our congratulations. They had just been shelled and had lost twenty men. In the fighting round and in the town they hadn't lost one.

O'Connor, Phillips, Cooper and myself went off together. The first thing we noticed was the open *pissoirs*; the second, that some side streets were marked 'Off limits to all Ranks.'

* Bennett replaced me as medical orderly.

'Flipping red-caps don't waste much time,' said Phillips.

We walked down one of the streets. A girl waved from a window. Phillips slipped into the house. We roared encouragement under the window.

'Yerrah, I'd be there myself if I wasn't a married man!'

'Don't give us that!' said Cooper. 'You're just saving it up.'

At the bottom of the main street we found some gardens overlooking the plains. We could see for miles. An Italian joined us. When he found I spoke French he really opened up.

'*Voila!*' he exclaimed, pointing at a hill half lost in the haze, '*Assisi!*'

I looked at him blankly.

'*Mais Assisi! San Francesco!*'

'*Ah, oui. Les Animaux.*'

'*Si, si! Il faux que vous visiter! Assisi est la perle d'Umbrie!*'

'Come on, Alec,' said Cooper. 'We'll be late for the show.'

I said goodbye to the Italian, promising him that I would visit Assisi, then went off with the others to see Bing Crosby and Bob Hope.

I never did get to Assisi. Bing Crosby had the edge on St. Francis, and the fountain beat them both. I spent hours there, just sitting and listening. I felt safe. I was a bit afraid of Assisi. So far I'd coped with fighting better than I'd hoped. I didn't want to meet anything that might weaken me. Putting it another way I was afraid of anything coming between me and the Company, afraid of losing the love and support I had found there. This attitude held good for sex, too. I was still a virgin. At Taranto, whilst riflemen were hiring girls for tins of bully, I lay in the grass daydreaming of those who did it for love. But I made no attempt to look for them.

Sometimes O'Connor would join me with a friend of his from Five Platoon, a Jew of Polish extraction called Zwolski. O'Connor called him Smith for short, and was always teasing him about what the Germans would do to him if they ever caught him. Zwolski had a blend of sensitivity and toughness I envied. The three of us sat and talked about the war. I can't remember what we said, except that it would have upset the generals.

The war was leaving us behind. The enemy no longer shelled Perugia. The Guards had occupied our hill without opposition. Its reverse slope had been thick with German dead. They had also found a dead signaller belonging to the Company.

Towards the end of the week we could no longer hear any guns. The Platoon's administrative changes were by no means so quiet. Our fifteen-hundred-weight driver got himself transferred to Company Headquarters. A fight for his job, always a plum one but now vintage – drivers didn't go into action – developed between O'Connor and two other Desert men. O'Connor played his age and won. I got the Tommy I'd promised myself but no new beret. The Quartermaster had berets in stock but as they weren't regimental pattern he refused to issue them. Mr. Simmonds, who had been wounded up the hill – typically he had told nobody about this – returned from hospital. This enabled Meadows to go on short leave to Perugia.

On June 28th Major Dunkerley's wound reopened and he went back to hospital. On the 30th a Captain Kendall took over the Company. We left the villa the same day, and harboured near Lake Trasimene.

Next morning Captain Kendall introduced himself to the Company. It was an impressive debut. Kendall, a wiry man with a skin-and-bone face, had been seconded from the Reconnaissance Corps. His uniform looked off the peg; those of our two previous commanders had been impeccably cut. As had their attitude to us. Like kindly squires they surveyed us from the heights. Kendall didn't survey anyone. Gathering us round him with a wave of his hand he gave us a most encouraging report of how the fighting was going and how we were likely to fit into it.

The Company stayed in the wood for three days. In the mornings we practised stalking. By a remarkable coincidence Mr. Simmonds dropped his pipe and I found it, and the same day I dropped mine, and he found it. He handed it over without a smile. 'I believe this is yours,' he said. With O'Connor and most of the others he relaxed. At times he even laughed. With me he maintained a chilly severity. I had met this sort of thing before. Not many officers felt at ease with a rifleman from the same background as themselves. They seemed afraid of not being able to maintain the proper distance between ranks. The pipe-finding amused O'Connor. 'You make a good pair, you two,' he said. 'I never met two more absent-minded fellows.' Mr. Simmonds had the edge on me. At times he still called us 'Six Platoon', its number in Tunisia.

being able to maintain the proper distance between ranks. The pipe-finding amused O'Connor. 'You make a good pair, you two,' he said. 'I never met two more absent-minded fellows.' Mr. Simmonds had the edge on me. At times he still called us 'Six Platoon', its number in Tunisia.

The evening before the Company left harbour Phillips and Gibson were made lance-corporals and everybody was issued with green camouflaged smocks. Our pale khaki-drill, excellent camouflage in the Desert, now stuck out like a range-target. German snipers had picked off so many men – two of them, officers with our 1st Battalion, had been contemporaries of mine at Radley – that G.H.Q.'s ponderous Think machine had belatedly decided on a variation of the German camouflage suit, something the Germans had been wearing for years. The smock certainly gave us a sense of protection and in a curious way mine made me feel I had turned professional.

7
SIX MEN AND A SPANDAU

We spent most of next day covering twenty miles.
The advance seemed to be slowing down. Some of
the 78th Division, pulling out for a rest, reassured us.

'They're on the run!' they shouted.

We were just harbouring when Meadows arrived
back from leave. If he had come by parachute he could
hardly have surprised us more. We had grown used to
moving in convoy, and being unable to overtake.

'We've had quite a time,' he said. 'When we got to
our *casa* the family was sitting down to dinner. And
who do you think was with them? "Topper" Brown!'

''e's on the trot!'* said Baker.

Meadows nodded.

'So we said "Hullo, 'Topper'," and he said "Hullo,
blokes," and we all sat down to dinner. When we'd
finished "Topper" gets up and says cheerio. We
wished him luck. The next thing we heard an engine
starting up. My girl rushes to the window – screams
her head off. "Topper" had pinched our Jeep. All our
stuff was on board – rifles, equipment, blankets, the
lot. Pete's trying to cover up the Jeep. I'm doing the
rest.'

* Slang for 'He's a deserter'.

101

Later, Meadows asked me if I would translate a letter to his girl into French, as she didn't speak English. I had some fun doing it.

The Brigade were moving in on some hills south of Arezzo. Fusiliers holding forward positions had picked up a dozen deserters in forty-eight hours, and Divisional Intelligence reported that partisans patrolling the hills had only seen one defence post – six men and a Spandau. The Divisional Commander had decided to commit the whole Brigade, just in case.

It sounded pretty good. But an hour before we were due to move Coke disappeared. Baker went looking for him with a Tommy. When we did move Sullivan was missing as well. His desertion gave me the same guilty feeling as I had had at Capua.

As we bumped over ploughed fields – the Germans had 'blown' the road – we heard the crash of bursting shells. The convoy halted. When the shelling stopped we drove on into a fog of cordite. There was a lot of hammering going on. The cordite lifted. I saw men stripped to the waist wrestling with the girders and banging home bolts like machines slightly out of control. In the background an officer was directing a stretcher-party. The sappers were building a Bailey under fire. I thanked God I wasn't one of them.

We harboured a mile beyond the bridge. In the morning we saw that only a line of trees separated us from the lee of the Arezzo hills. There were three of them, great pot-bellied brutes nearly four thousand feet high, and Monte Lignano, the Company's objective was the one farthest away.

Sullivan turned up as we were having breakfast. He had had second thoughts about deserting. Mr.

Simmonds let him off with a warning.

O'Connor and I spent the morning in a villa that had been a German H.Q. Someone else had beaten us to it, but they had left some pickings. I found a Venetian scent-bottle and a German Army magazine called *Sud Front*. This had the quality and to some extent content of *The London Illustrated News*. It included illustrated articles on Florence and the Pisa-Rimini or Gothic Line, a wicked-looking defence system being built in the mountains beyond Florence (this must have made comforting reading for the retreating Germans). For good measure there was a two-page spread of luscious German nudes. Someone knew what to give the troops. The 8th Army's equivalent to *Sud Front*, the *Crusader*, was so bad no one in the Platoon bothered to read it. We used it for 'bumf'. The German officers knew how to look after themselves, too, judging by the number of empty champagne bottles lying round the dustbins. One bottle, Bollinger 1938, had printed on it 'For export to England'. Across this was stamped '*Reservé pour le Wehrmacht*'. O'Connor found a box that fitted the scent-bottle and had it packed and posted within the hour. They were presents for my mother, and because of this perhaps I felt as if part of myself was going home. I needed a bit of comfort. O'Connor's eyes mirrored my own doubts. How would I get on without him?

We had just finished lunch when two companies of the 5th moved through our lines. At once the enemy started to shell us. We took to the ditch, cursing the 5th. The shelling kept us there until it was time – 2 p.m. – to start our own march.

The 5th were approaching Monte Lignano, the Battalions' joint objective, across fields. Captain Kendall led us along a road running parallel with the hills. The hedgerow wasn't quite high enough to hide us completely so we used the 'Ostrich Walk', head and shoulders bent, the technique so deprecated by home-based P.T. instructors, who would have had us on our haunches doing something called the 'Cossack Crawl' (impracticable for anyone except a P.T. instructor). Through an occasional gap in the hedge I could see tanks half-way up Lignano. They were being heavily mortared but continued to crawl upwards. I guessed it must be a different regiment from the one that had turned tail at Perugia (it was). And then another heavy barrage came down over to the right, and nearer the summit. The 5th had been spotted.

The roadside was littered with leaflets. They depicted London in flames. 'This is the work of the V.1. When will the V.2 strike?' read the caption. I had an uneasy feeling that this wasn't just guff. For once German propaganda scored a bit.

The hedge shielded us from the enemy but not from the sun. 'Ostrich walking' in the nineties is an exhausting business. Captain Kendall halted us three times in two miles. At the last halt an Italian ran out of a house with a bucket of ice-cold water. I drank like an animal. As we moved off again one of Baker's section collapsed. Medical orderlies helped him away.

Directly after this we left the road, and began climbing a river-bed. Italians popped out of bushes like rabbits in the evening sun.

'*Viva gli Inglesi*!' they shouted. '*Abbasso i Tedeschi*!'

They paraded us triumphantly into a hamlet. The inhabitants made it seem much bigger than it was. But as they swarmed round us we saw we were all in full view of Lignano. Pointing at the mountains we shouted 'Tedeschi! Boom! Boom!' But the villagers couldn't or, more likely, wouldn't understand. Nothing was going to spoil *their* liberation. We began to manhandle them off the street. The villagers protested, loudly. Was this the way liberators behaved? What sort of people were the English anyway? But then the Germans obliged with a couple of mortar-bombs. The street emptied with almost comical suddenness. The Platoon split up. My half took shelter in a stable, alone with a dozen villagers and two mules. As we squatted down a girl ran in screaming. She was covered in blood. The other women screamed in sympathy. Meadows examined her and indicated it was only a flesh wound. But something the girl said set the women screaming louder than ever. Then the girl had hysterics. In the confined space the noise was unnerving. I retreated towards the mules. They hadn't blinked an eyelid. As I patted them approvingly one of the villagers tried Meadows in French. He called me over to interpret. It seemed that the injured woman's mother had been blown down by a bomb, and was unable to move.

'I'll go and get her,' I said.

Anything to get away from the wailing.

Humphreys came with me. V. found the old woman sitting under a table in a room covered with broken glass – the bomb had blown in the windows. She stared up at us without speaking.

'Come on, Ma!' said Humphreys invitingly.

But when he went to help her up she spat at him like a snake. Then we both grabbed an arm. It took all our strength to move her. When we arrived at the stable the women screamed and the daughter had hysterics again. But after the mother had been enfolded, and nothing found wrong with her, the noise died down until we could even hear the mortaring.

The Germans kept it up for an hour. When they began to lose interest Mr. Simmonds dropped in and told Meadows to send someone to find a covered approach out of the village. Meadows raised his eyebrows at me. I nodded. As I ran into the open I felt a little drunk. It was my day. I didn't miss O'Connor at all. The road leading out of the village was flanked by stone walls eight feet high. I found a track that cut on to it, and within a few minutes the Company was once again moving up to Lignano.

The road ended half-way up the mountain. As we rested we watched the tanks being mortared. They were now on a ridge away to our left, about three-quarters way up, and judging from the gradient that was about as high as they would get. The Germans had stopped mortaring the 5th.

The upper half of Lignano was heavily wooded, and the ground itself a succession of banks and burrows. I soon lost all sense of time. The woods were dark, and only when they grew darker still did I realize how late it was. Soon after this we heard men moving downhill. Captain Kendall flung up a hand. Someone said something in English. It was the 5th. Their officers conferred with ours and I gathered we were taking over their position. According to our information both Battalions were to have been on the hill together. It was the first of several surprises.

The 5th left us a guide. After ten minutes he said he was lost. Captain Kendall was short and to the point. The guide slunk off. We moved forward cautiously, too concerned about ourselves to slang the 5th. A volley of rifle shots sent us flat. We had arrived. Mortars took up the challenge. I have confused memories of bombs bursting in the trees, of myself hacking at the ground, and of Captain Kendall crouching in front of me, head towards the enemy, like a pointer analysing the scent. It was too hot. After hanging on for ten minutes the Company moved another two hundred yards over to the left. We left the mortaring behind us.

Whilst the rest of the Company dug in Five Platoon went out on a fighting patrol. The crunch of bursting grenades made me wince, but the patrol returned safely, bringing a prisoner with them. They had surprised an enemy platoon dug-in round a farmhouse, and had killed or wounded several of them.

By dawn we were all well dug-in. Five Platoon were somewhere in front, Six Platoon on the right. The only thing we needed was water. Captain Kendall discussed the problem with Mr. Simmonds. I was very thirsty.

'I'll find some, sir,' I said.

The officers looked at me.

'All right,' said Captain Kendall. 'But mind you keep under cover.'

I assured him I would, then waltzed down the hillside. My mood changed when I saw a thirty-yard clearing stretching right across the hillside. (We must have crossed it during the night but it hadn't registered.) And overlooking everything was a great pinnacle of rock. The Germans had certainly shot us up from there. If I crossed the clearing they'd spot me. If I didn't the Company wouldn't get any water. I decided that water mattered more than keeping under cover, and that I would walk, and not run, across the gap – I wasn't going to give the Germans a laugh if I could help it. Taking a deep breath I stepped into the open. As I did so I glared at the pinnacle – and kept glaring. Half-way across I pulled a face. The Germans kept quiet.

A hundred yards farther down the hill I found an ice-cold spring. The water had a delicious flavour, and I drank pints of it. The return journey was equally uneventful. When I reported the lack of cover to Captain Kendall he remarked that it couldn't be helped, and told me to take one man from each platoon down to the spring.

I took Humphreys first. We crossed the clearing – Humphreys seemed unaware of its significance and I saw no point in explaining – and gossiped our way down the hill. When we came to a second clearing I pulled up.

'You know I don't remember coming this far.'

'Oh?' said Humphreys suspiciously.

'Still it was just off the path, so we can't miss it.'

We walked into the open and at once I sensed something overhanging us. I looked up. We were right under the pinnacle.

'Good Lord! The Germans are up there.'

Humphreys shook his head at me.

'You're a lad, you are!'

I burst out laughing. We about turned and walked back into the trees. There we found another path a few feet below the one we were on. The spring was between the two.

Walking about under the nose of the enemy gave me quite a kick. As I guided the remaining water-carriers I made up travel captions. 'Conducted tours of the Appenines. Travellers travel entirely at their own risk' was one. When Jeeps arrived at the spring loaded with hot stew I had to remind myself I wasn't in England on a scheme (a mild but persistent smell of death helped). After washing down the stew with a lot more water I curled up in my trench and went to sleep.

I was woken by a roar of explosions. Paralysed with fear I listened to a mortar-barrage sweep over the Company. Five Platoon's Brens opened up. Forcing myself to look over the parapet I saw Mr. Simmonds jump out of his trench.

'Six Platoon!' he yelled. 'Come to the help of your friends!'

None of us moved. For a moment Mr. Simmonds stood upright in a pelt of shrapnel, then he jumped back into his trench. Humphreys, who had dug himself a 'lean-to' trench, caught my eye. We grinned.

The firing stopped. So did the mortaring. The stretcher-bearers began to evacuate the wounded. One of them, a queer little chap who never stopped talking, had been wounded whilst giving first-aid. As he limped down the slope he turned round and shouted 'Stick it, lads!' We shouted back. Passionately. For once his words had been exactly right.

Five Platoon had been attacked by ten Germans. They had shot the lot. Their own casualties had been one man killed and four wounded, all from the mortaring. I was glad of that. If we had responded to Mr. Simmonds's gesture we must have suffered casualties from the mortaring ourselves, and for no reason. Just the same, I felt a little ashamed of our 'blind eye'.

The Company awaited another attack. None came. I began dosing myself with thoughts as 'Perhaps they've had enough' and 'Perhaps they've run out of mortar-bombs'. I didn't believe it for a moment but they helped balance the idea of being bayoneted in the stomach.

They hit us at dusk. For two minutes the whole hillside shook with one continuous roll of explosions. I cowered in my trench, fighting for control. As the barrage died down I heard Captain Kendall shout 'Abandon positions, "D" Company!'

I stepped out of my trench, listening to the crunch of feet moving through the undergrowth. It was difficult to believe there were that many men left. Familiar faces passed me with a wry grin or a brief word. None of the Platoon had been touched. As I turned to follow them I ran into an emergency stretcher-party in need of a fourth man. They were carrying a wounded rifleman in a camouflage jacket. I took a corner of it, and we began working our way along the hillside. The path wasn't wide enough to take two of us abreast, so we had to walk on the slope. The rifleman was wounded in the stomach. He bled like a pig. Morphia had only dulled his pain, and he rolled about in the jacket moaning softly, his red hair accentuating the pallor of his face.

'He can't live,' I thought.

The smell of the wound sickened me, and only the strain of the carrying prevented me from vomiting. When we reached the new Company positions – two hundred yards or so farther over to the left – two men with a stretcher took over from us. We looked down at our man, wished him luck. None of us thought he would survive the journey downhill.*

I found the Platoon crouching fifteen yards below the ridge of the hill.

'Captain Kendall thinks they'll attack any moment,' whispered Swallow. 'He's asked for a counter-barrage.'

As he spoke guns opened up in the valley. A whoosh of shells screamed overhead – a few feet overhead – and landed just the other side of the ridge. Any moment I expected one to fall short but none did.† The silence that followed the barrage was even more terrifying. As I stared at the ridge a knife-like pain seared my stomach. I doubled up, and the pain explained itself. Crawling to a hollow a few feet below me I let my trousers down.

'How not to be caught by the enemy,' I thought, and grinned ruefully. That would teach me to pig spring water.

As soon as I got back to my position I had another spasm. As I turned towards the hollow Mr. Simmonds whispered, 'There's no need to be so modest.'

'Does he want me to sit in it?' I thought, and kept crawling.

As far as the rest of the Platoon was concerned the

---

* He was back with the Company within two months.
† Not on us, but 'A' Company, on our left, had two men killed.

Germans had taken a back seat. My antics had snapped the tension for them as much as it had for me. And when it was over the silence had changed sides. The odds on an enemy attack lengthened every minute. Captain Kendall leaned towards Mr. Simmonds.

'I don't think they'll come now,' he said.

The two officers got together. Then Mr. Simmonds talked with Meadows, who told Swallow and me to report to Captain Kendall.

'He's taking you on patrol,' he said.

'Is he now?' I thought. 'That's the last bloody straw.'

There were five others on the patrol. Captain Kendall looked us over.

'You have been recommended as reliable men in a most unreliable Company,' he said.

He let the words sink in.

'Reliable men?' I thought. 'Christ, if he only knew how reliable I feel.'

'We are going back to the old positions to identify and bury our dead,' continued the Company Commander. 'The enemy may be waiting for us. If they are we'll shoot them up and then withdraw.'

I made a face at that. Corporal Bailey grinned at me. It was good to think of him being on the patrol. He had the reputation of being the finest N.C.O. in the Company, and one of the quietest. He was also remarkably good-looking. I hero-worshipped him.

'We'll start right away. In extended line,' said Captain Kendall.

The patrol fanned out on either side of him, and off we went. I had never liked night-patrols even when training. I could never see a thing. Once I had been on the tail-end of one patrol hunting another over a Yorkshire moor. After we had blundered around for an hour I called out to the man in front of me. He turned round, and we stared at each other in amazement. I had joined up with the 'enemy' patrol.

I was prepared for night-blindness. The loneliness was a shock. Instead of eighty men we were eight. And I felt just about ten times less secure. The noise we made didn't help. In places we had to break through the undergrowth. I remembered a training lecture. 'On a night-patrol silence really is golden,' the officer had said.

As we neared the old positions we slowed down.

'They're waiting for us,' I thought. 'Will I have the guts to fire back?'

We halted. The top half of the positions were lit up by the moon. Beyond them, the pinnacle. In the moonlight it seemed terrifyingly close. I could even see the cracks on the rock. Was it thirty yards away? Or fifty? We crept forward. In the third trench we found a dead rifleman. Whilst Captain Kendall removed his identity disc one of the patrol whispered, 'He was the last of six brothers – all killed in the war.' We covered him with the earth from his own parapet. After identifying and burying five more men – all from Six Platoon, who now existed in name only – Corporal Bailey told the Company Commander that one of his platoon was somewhere at the top of the slope.

'I and Corporal Bailey are going to look for the body,' said Captain Kendall. 'The rest of you take up positions here.'

113

They disappeared over the top of the slope. Then we heard a rasping noise. They were dragging the body over the ground. The Germans couldn't fail to hear.

'Christ!' I thought. 'They'll be burying us in a minute.'

What was the point of risking eight lives for a corpse? I reproached myself for lack of chivalry, but it didn't help. The Germans had some to spare. They left us in peace. When the man was buried Captain Kendall turned back to us.

'Right,' he said. 'We will stay here until first light. The Germans may send a patrol out. If they do we will ambush them.'

'You bastard!' I muttered to myself.

As I wrapped myself round a tree – it was getting chilly – some heavy machine-gunning broke out from the neighbouring hill, Monte Maggio. The 1st were on it. The firing continued for nearly two hours. I slipped into my 'half-sleep' and Swallow tried unsuccessfully to catch me unconscious. By two o'clock I was wide awake with cold. Towards dawn I began wondering if Captain Kendall had any more surprises for us. He hadn't. When we arrived back with the Company he remarked, 'You've all done very well.'

This somehow made me feel as cool and capable as himself. If I had a tail I would have wagged it. But when I rejoined the Platoon and found them all comfortably dug-in, I didn't feel so good. My previous trench had been full of tree-roots. This time I hit rock. The more I dug the bigger it grew. My swearing attracted Humphreys, who stood round offering useless advice. Eventually the rock took up the whole of the bottom of the trench – still only a foot deep. I had the choice of digging a new trench – a fourth one – or seeing if I could dig round the rock – sidewards, then downwards. I decided to try digging round. An exploratory dig proved 'soft'. When the gap seemed big enough to use I tried to squeeze in – and failed. I went berserk, attacking the gap as if it were a living enemy, then hurled myself into the trench. This time I made it. Face-upwards I lay looking at the sky. Grinning. Then I went to sit up. I couldn't move. The gap held me like a vice. I had Bateman-like visions of 'The man who got stuck in his own slit-trench'. Was I to call for help and have the whole Platoon kill themselves laughing? As I lay waiting for some miraculous alternative the sky was blotted out by Captain Kendall.

'What on earth are you doing down there?' he said.

'I'm stuck, sir.'

Smiling he grabbed me by the shoulder and yanked me out of the trench. Humphreys looked at me suspiciously but didn't twig what had happened. I sat down and ate a whole tin of Spam. I also counted my blisters. I had eighteen on my right hand; those on my pads were three deep.

From my trench I had a fine view of the valley road up which we had marched, and, at right angles to this, the nearest flank of Monte Maggio. Baker told me about the night-battle I had heard.

'The 1st got counter-attacked. The Teds rolled up two companies, and got as far as Battalion H.Q. Whilst the Companies sorted themselves out the cooks and batmen took on the Teds. Then the

Companies pushed them right back.'

'We could learn a thing or two from them,' said Mr. Simmonds.

Near the top of Maggio there was a patch of dug-outs. As I watched them through field-glasses the Germans began shelling a village on the valley road. There must have been at least a hundred guns firing.

'Those six men and their Spandau aren't doing too bad,' remarked Humphreys.

'I wish we 'ad some of those Intelligence wallahs up 'ere,' said Lance-Corporal Phillips.

Not long after the barrage lifted I spotted a cloud of dust moving up the valley road. It was a convoy of twenty-five-pounders.

'The guns are coming up!'

Baker snatched the glasses. I watched the ant-size trailers race through the village and turn into a field at the foot of Lignano.

'They must be bloody daft!' said Baker.

I took the glasses back from him. The gunners ran round getting the guns into position. Humphreys took the glasses. The Platoon watched in silence, waiting for the enemy gunners – who waited for ours. The twenty-fives fired one round. The enemy answered with a barrage of such intensity that the whole field disappeared in smoke. When it cleared the gunners were moving out. They left behind a col-lection of guns and trailers, some of which were burning. We cursed whoever had ordered them up.

In the meantime the enemy gunners were cele-brating. They fired happily at nothing until a stray shell hit our A.D.S.,* a chapel clearly marked with a

*Advanced Dressing Station for wounded.

116

red cross. Someone inside began ringing the bell. It drew the attention of the German gunners' observer, but not in the way intended. He simply directed *all* the guns on to the chapel. Dumb with horror we watched it struck again and again. The bell continued to ring. The rate of fire increased. Bits fell off the chapel. It seemed only a matter of time before the whole building collapsed. We listened to the bell as if our lives depended on it. God and the Devil suddenly seemed very real. When the shelling died down the bell was still ringing. It continued to ring for minutes after the last shell. We were too moved to say anything. We just grunted, and found pieces of kit that needed attention. But what had happened on the hill no longer seemed so meaningless.

As if to show us we weren't forgotten the enemy began probing for us with mortars. One or two bombs came over every few minutes. This sort of thing was known as harassing fire, and I found it particularly so after lunch (hot stew brought up by foot) when I could have done with some sleep. Instead I looked back on the previous twenty-four hours. It was now clear why the enemy hadn't shot me. They had been after bigger game. I didn't feel happy about having led them to it.

The enemy kept up the harassing fire all night. I got no sleep at all. After breakfast they stopped firing but although I was beginning to feel the cumulative effect of fatigue I couldn't relax. The silence worried me. It worried Captain Kendall, too. He established an outpost just below the ridge. When a group of us took over from Five Platoon we found Captain Kendall there himself, head cocked on one side, feeling for the Germans.

'I think we'll have a man up there,' he said, pointing to the top of the ridge.

A rifleman named Ellis crawled up the ridge.

'Can you see anything?' asked Captain Kendall.

'No, sir.'

'Go a bit farther forward.'

Ellis did so. A mortar-bomb burst on the ridge. Ellis jumped up – and another bomb landed at his feet, showering him with cordite. He raced down the ridge, his face contorted with shock. Captain Kendall caught him like a rugger ball.

'You're all right, Ellis,' he said quietly. 'You're all right.'

Ellis's face lost its fear. He sat down, and Baker knelt beside him.

'We'll have to scrub that O.P.,' said Captain Kendall. 'Some tanks are trying to come up and have a shoot. I hope they make it.'

I noticed that Cooper now looked a good deal more shaky than Ellis. I grinned at him, and he managed one back.

Two Shermans duly turned up on our left and shelled the pinnacle. For two hours they kept the enemy very quiet. But as soon as they trundled away the enemy mortarmen resumed their harassing fire. It grew heavier as the day went on. Only the fact that our trenches were well apart – in the old positions they had been much too close – kept our casualties down to two wounded. (This made a total of seven killed and twenty-odd wounded. The Platoon's luck still held. We took good care not to talk about it.) The Company was to be relieved that night, and I wondered if the Germans had got wind of this. The nearer the relief the more pessimistic I grew. This time it was our turn to get caught. They'd stick us like pigs. I was busy writing off the Company when Mr. Simmonds looked down at me.

'I want you to go and lead in the relieving Company,' he said. 'They should be arriving quite soon.'

Jumping out of my trench I raced across the hillside. Once clear of the mortaring I slowed down. No bayonets for me. Then I stopped dead. Overhanging the path were the remains of a tree. Mortarbombs had ripped it apart, white wood stuck out like broken bones. Bark curled back like burnt flesh. It was a corpse, not a tree. Instinctively I got off the path and found another lower down. As I drew level with the tree a mortar-bomb landed on top of it. I ran. The Germans must have had a listening-post out.

I waited for the relieving Company in a conveniently placed hollow. When they arrived I told their leading officers what was happening, and led them to our positions. It was then that I noticed a rifleman carrying what looked like a camp-bed. It couldn't be.

'What on earth have you got there?' I asked him.

'Company Commander's bed,' said the batman, as if it was the most natural thing in the world to be carrying.

'Is this the first time you've been in action in Italy?' I asked.

'Yes.'

'Well, good luck, chum.'

'You'll need it,' I thought.

Four Platoon led the Company downhill. We were

119

a couple of hundred yards past the spring when the enemy mortared it heavily. That was that, or so it seemed. But when we approached the village at the foot of Lignano Captain Kendall ordered the Company to march in threes. During the day the enemy had shelled the village a dozen times. The last had been whilst we were on our way down Lignano. The air was still heavy with cordite fumes. The Platoon muttered angrily but, although I grumbled as much as anyone, I couldn't help admiring Captain Kendall's technique. If anyone was going to make us a 'reliable Company' it would be him.

The trucks met us outside the village. One of the cooks was there, too. He gave us some tea. It was watery, sugarless, and tasted of mess-tin, but I've never enjoyed tea so much. I fell asleep as soon as I got into the truck, and only woke up when we bumped into harbour.

8

CAPTAIN KENDALL
IN COMMAND

Once again the sun woke me, only this time it was a really hot one. When I opened my eyes I had a shock. I was staring straight at Lignano. We were right opposite it. I looked round wildly. Baker saw me.

'Don't get a bubble on, Alec,' he said.

'They can see the lot of us!'

'Now look,' said Baker patiently. 'It's ten o'clock. They've 'ad five hours to stonk us. We're nicely out of range.'

Reassured, I got out of bed. When I looked at my shaving mirror I had another shock. Four days' dirt, beard, and cordite had left only my eyes familiar. I grinned – and my teeth flashed like a coalman's.

On my way to breakfast I met Coke, under escort.

'Enjoy yourself?' he said nastily.

An hour later he went up before the C.O. He came back grinning ear to ear.

'Got a court-martial!' he said, as if it was a decoration.

'What did you say to the C.O., Cokey?' asked Humphreys curiously.

'I told 'im I 'ad a feeling I shouldn't go up no more hills.'

We tittered. Baker was furious.

'You'll get three years!' he roared.

Coke grinned.

'And I'll be 'ere when you're pushing up the daisies.'

Baker grabbed him by the throat.

'Say that again and I'll shoot you me fucking self!'

Coke went white.

'I got my rights as a prisoner,' he muttered.

'Better let him go, Titch,' said Meadows.

Baker did so, and Coke crawled into his bivouac.

Military procedure decreed that we had to look after Coke until the Military Police took him off our hands – and they had to fetch him, we couldn't deliver the goods ourselves. For this, and perhaps another reason, Baker's offer to drive him back to Corps H.Q. was not accepted. It meant that we had to guard him day and night. The idea of a night-guard – for ordinary purposes the cooks and drivers mounted guard whilst the Company was resting – got under everybody's skin.

The harbour was half a mile on the other side of the road up which we had approached Lignano. In the afternoon a Jeep used the road and the enemy gunners opened fire. Their O.P must have found us most tantalizing. The hills themselves remained silent. It was hard to believe they were full of Germans. Only at night did the slopes come alive. Nervous bursts of Spandau tracered the dark, and Lignano's pinnacle, silhouetted against a luminous sky, looked like a witch's hat.

In the morning we heard that the Company who had relieved us had been attacked the same night as they had relieved us. They had withdrawn to fresh positions. I wondered what had happened to the camp-bed. Divisional Intelligence had had second thoughts about the strength of the enemy, who were now considered to be 'picked elements of a Panzer Grenadier Division'. The 1st were withdrawn from Maggio (the day after their night battle their stretcher-bearers had teamed up with the enemy's, and after picking up the wounded they had all sat down together for a smoke), prior to an attack by the 2nd New Zealand Division and our own Guards' Brigade. In the meantime 'D' Company chalked up two local victories of their own.

Captain Kendall had recommended an officer for the M.C. His platoon had sent Corporal Bailey to protest. He told O'Connor and me exactly what had happened.

'When I got in there,' he said, 'Captain Kendall said, "Hullo, Corporal, what's on your mind?" "Well, sir," I said, "before you took over something pretty bad happened." I wasn't sure how to go on but old Kendall smiled and said, "I'm listening." So I said, "When we were up the hill at Perugia Mr. Driver just sat in his trench. He didn't do a thing, not even when chaps were wounded." "I see," said Captain Kendall. "I'm very glad you told me."'

Captain Kendall cancelled the recommendation and had the officer transferred to another battalion.

The other victory was at the expense of the new C.S.M., 'Bombhead' Rogers (our old C.S.M. was due for repatriation). His reputation of being a loud-mouthed prick arrived before him, and he certainly lived up to it. As soon as he had taken over he walked round the harbour making unnecessary noises. He then withdrew to his tent and made a lot more. This proved his undoing. It didn't need a 'grapevine' to hear he intended introducing P.T. before breakfast. The Company were appalled. P.T. at any time was bad enough. P.T. before breakfast was the end. Five Platoon were the first to react. They charged round the harbour waving their P.T. shorts and chanting 'No P.T.! No P.T.!' The rest of us followed on. Round and round we went, reserving our loudest shouts for the C.S.M.'s tent. Like the great Achilles 'Bombhead' Rogers stayed inside. And kept quiet. The next day Captain Kendall told him he thought P.T. before breakfast unnecessary. The Company was already scheduled for four hours' training each day, and that would kept it in condition. Captain Kendall's stock soared.

An article in *The Eighth Army News* got our backs up in another way. Roosevelt had suggested to Churchill that the United States should provide all the land forces for the Pacific sector. Churchill had turned this down. 'We can't let your chaps have all the fun,' he had said. This infuriated us. War may have been fun to him; it wasn't to us. Churchill replaced Lady 'D-Day Dodgers' Astor as our V.I.P. Aunt Sally.

On July 14th – five days after we had withdrawn from Lignano – the Kiwis moved up the Line. One unit harboured near the Company and some of us went over to say hullo. It was a strange meeting. The Kiwis seemed far older and more mature than ourselves, and we must have seemed babes-in-arms to them. They made no attempt to cover up that they were on the eve of a big attack. They hardly said a word. We wished them luck and left.

The Kiwis' attack was due to go in at 1 a.m. the next morning. We had heard that their support barrage would be something rather special. It was. The gunners opened up an hour after dark. They used twenty-fives', mediums' and 4·2 mortars. (The Germans called these 'Whispering Death'.) Shells landed at the rate of between twenty and thirty *a second*. The hills were lit up from top to bottom. None of us had ever seen anything like it. For a while we just stood and watched, mesmerized by the bursting shells. When we did speak it was 'Fuck their luck!' and 'Poor old Teds!' This was a 'sharp end' to end all 'sharp ends'.

The barrage continued until shortly before one o'clock (the gunners told us that they fired more shells than had been used for the preliminary barrage at Alamein). The attack was completely successful. The New Zealanders captured Lignano and Maggio after hand-to-hand fighting – they claimed forty Germans killed on Lignano alone – and the Guards slipped round the back of the hills without meeting any resistance. The Kiwis reported that our dead buried on Lignano had been blown out of their graves by the intensity of the barrage, and that they had reburied them. They also handed over some notes found on the body of a German Intelligence Officer. Dated July 6th, 'D' Company's first full day on Lignano they read – in translation: 'A company of Riflemen have dug in below us. Judging from their scruffy appearance they belong to the 3rd Battalion.' This delighted us.

The day after the attack the tanks, supported by the

10th, attacked Arezzo. The enemy rearguards withdrew after token resistance. Next morning 'D' company joined in the advance. Just before we left harbour I found my best pair of trousers – my 'Florence' trousers – were missing. Humphreys was suspiciously concerned about it.

After driving through the outskirts of Arezzo, which were badly knocked about, we spent the afternoon in a Brigade 'car park' north of the city. Then we pushed off by ourselves, harbouring in a snug little field enclosed by low hills. Even the track we entered by was covered by a wood. It was love at first sight. Within the hour we had made the field our own private property. It was a home, not a harbour. And we celebrated with a sing-song – Five Platoon had picked up a piano in Arezzo – that began after dinner and went on till midnight. One of the dispatch-riders had a pleasant Irish tenor, and he led us in 'When Irish eyes are smiling', 'Danny Boy', 'Galway Bay', 'If I had my way' and other old favourites. Captain Kendall and Mr. Simmonds, the only officers in the Company, enjoyed themselves as much as we did. The evening ended with a tremendous performance of 'The Gippo Anthem'.

> 'Now we're all black bastards
> But we do love our king!
> Shufti cush Allah kif Allah u Bardin!
> If you want to have Farida
> You have got to have Farouk!
> Stanis swoi Amarya shufti cush Bardin!'

In the morning Six Platoon – reinforced during the rest – were told to stand by. A squadron of tanks

126

were attacking a village called Laterino a few miles from the harbour. They might need support.

I lay down in the shade of the three-tonner, head against the wheel, and looked dreamily into the wood. Whoever else was going on the patrol I wasn't. A rush of feet cut short the dream. As I sat up an explosion sent shrapnel flying over the truck.

'Mortars!' I thought.

'Get your weapons, Four Platoon!' yelled Mr. Simmonds.

I jumped up, grabbed my Tommy, and ran into the wood – two yards from the truck. Dropping flat I faced the field. I couldn't see anything except the truck. Several men rushed round it and fled past me.

'They've jumped us!' I thought.

Mr. Simmonds and Phillips dropped beside me. As we waited for the enemy to charge Captain Kendall shouted 'All right, "D" Company! False alarm!'

Mystified, we stepped into the field and bumped into Meadows.

'One of those twots in Six Platoon,' he said. 'Fixing a grenade in his belt.* No one hurt.'

Minutes later the tank's squadron-commander wirelessed Captain Kendall. They had run into trouble from bazookas and had lost three tanks. Although he didn't think there was much opposition he suggested the whole Company came along. Captain Kendall agreed.

The Platoon began dressing. I was trying to make up my mind whether the grenade incident was a good omen or not when Cooper sat down and burst

* A dangerous, if handy, way of carrying grenades.

into tears.

'I can't take any more!' he said. 'I can't!'

Baker squatted down beside him.

'You'll be all right, Sammy,' he said. 'I'll look after you.'

"'e'll look after you!' said Coke, from outside his bivouac. 'Bring you back when you've 'ad it!'

Baker jumped up and rushed at him. Meadows stepped in between.

'He's not worth it, Titch.'

The rest of us looked at Coke as if killing was too good for him. He crawled backwards into his bivouac, like a tortoise going into its shell. In the meantime Captain Kendall had joined the Platoon.

'What's the trouble, Sergeant?' he asked.

Meadows explained. Captain Kendall knelt down on one knee.

'Look, Cooper,' he said. 'Give it a go. If we run into trouble and you can't cope you can come back. All right?'

Cooper stopped crying, and nodded.

'Good lad!'

Captain Kendall stood up and smiled.

'They say we're coming out of the Line at Florence. We should be there pretty soon.'

We answered that with a chorus of 'Just the job, sir!', 'Roll on Florence!' and 'Where's my Melody* suit!'

As soon as Captain Kendall had gone the C.S.M. arranged to take Coke on a 'patrol'. Luckily for him Mr. Simmonds got wind of the idea, and squashed it.

† The 'Melody' was a Cairo cabaret.

The Company had the curious experience of marching for half a mile or more along a lane lined with tanks and their crews. These amused themselves by presenting arms and shouting 'Here they come! Hooray!' We gave them a boxer's salute. All it needed was someone to play 'The Entry of the Gladiators'. A group of three officers from an armoured-car regiment – The King's Dragoon Guards, known to us for regimental reasons as 'The King's Dancing Girls' – grinned at us in a conspiratorial way that I found quite delightful. Mixed up in our counter-clowning was an intense pride. I had never felt so conscious of my regiment as I was then. This was the way to risk one's life. There was no King or Country about it – it was the regiment. And I wouldn't have changed places with anyone.

Soon after we had left our 'supporters' we passed two Battalion Bren carriers. Both had broken down and their crews were working on them.

'Want a push!' we shouted.

'That's our mortar support, that is!' said Phillips in disgust.

'Dear, oh dear!' said Humphreys. 'To think we 'ave to rely on you chaps.'

As we left them behind Page shouted 'Send you a postcard when we get there!'

Leaving the lane we entered a wood. A steep path led to a river. Although it wasn't wide it had a sharp current. We found some stepping-stones and waded across. Page missed his footing and went up to his neck. On the other side we were met by two civilians who volunteered to lead us through an anti-personnel* minefield between us and the tanks. Captain Kendall accepted the offer, telling the civilians to keep to the rear of the Company until we neared the minefield. He then formed the Company into threes. What was he up to now? We moved off up a track. Ahead of us was a ridge. When we breasted it I gasped. The ground to the left of the track fell away steeply. Below us was a valley – two miles across it the tanks, strung out on a hillside like giant snails. We were a tit-bit for anyone between us and the tanks. I waited for Captain Kendall to order us into single file. He kept marching.

'Clay pigeons!' I muttered.

The Germans fired two shots. The Company went to ground as if it had been two hundred. Only Captain Kendall remained on his feet. A Spandau opened up. We clung to the ground as if it alone could save us. Captain Kendall walked slowly through the Company.

'Look at me,' he said quietly. 'They can't hit me. Look at me.'

We looked. He might have been taking a stroll in the sun. The Germans didn't hit him. His courage hit us. We got to our feet.

'Right!' shouted Captain Kendall. 'We will attack! Four Platoon on the left, Six on the right! Sergeant Meadows, there's a Honey-tank at Company rear H.Q. – send one of your sections back to guard it!'

Meadows signalled to Swallow. As the section drew away the Company deployed for the attack. The voices of the N.C.O.s rang out like bugles, the

Fn from p.129. * The Germans had two main types – the S-mine, a shrapnel-filled horror that sprang into the air when trodden on, exploding a few feet above ground, and the wooden Schu-mine, difficult to trace even with detectors but nothing like as deadly as the S-mine.

wing platoons bucketed into line, and the Company swept forward. It was beautifully done. As a model of deployment under fire – more Spandaus had opened up – it could hardly have been bettered. Coming from an apparently bomb-happy Company it was a revelation. I thanked our stars for Captain Kendall.

We found the Honey-tank – a small tank with, in this case, no turret – in front of a farmhouse. Whilst Swallow reported to the C.S.M. the rest of us lay down in front of the tank (the section had been reinforced by a rifleman called Roberts, who had been with the Platoon in the Desert, and one of the cooks). Whilst delighted at having missed the attack – we had talked about this all the way back to the farm – the idea of defending a tank puzzled us. Surely it should have been the other way round? The crackle of the tank's wireless stopped our discussion. We heard the ghostly voice of the squadron-commander reporting from the hillside. When he said 'I advise our small friends not to attack without our support' we nodded in approval. The Company was being mortared as well as Spandau-ed. The tanks would provide the right 'umbrella'. As another message came through a rifleman ran over the ridge and headed for the farm. He looked very shaky.

'C.S.M.!' he gasped.

We nodded towards the farmhouse. The runner dashed inside. A moment later the C.S.M. charged out.

'Where's that bloody runner?' he shouted.

'He went inside to look for you, sir,' said Swallow.

'Shit!' said the C.S.M. 'He gave me a message, then fucked off.'

131

''e must 'ave kept on running, sir,' said Gibson innocently.

'Wait till I get hold of him!' said the C.S.M.

As soon as he'd re-entered the farm we burst out laughing. We were still at it when another runner appeared. He was a replacement, very fat and out of condition. We watched him puff his way across the field, awed by the possibility of another home-run.

'Here's another runner, sir!' shouted Swallow.

The C.S.M. ran out to meet him.

'Captain Kendall says 'e's attacking at once, sir!' said the runner. ''e's not waiting for the tanks, and 'e wants Corporal Swallow's section to rejoin the Company for the attack.'

'Right!' said the C.S.M. 'Off you go!'

The runner ran back the same way as he had come. A disgusted section got to its feet.

'Why couldn't he wait for the tanks?' I said.

''e's too keen. That's 'is trouble,' said Gibson.

Automatically we got into line and began walking across the field, grumbling as we went. We were half-way when a Spandau opened up from close range. We fell flat, then slithered behind a ridge.

'We'll 'ave to find another way, Stan!' said Gibson.

Swallow nodded. We crawled back to the farm-house. An anxious-looking C.S.M. was waiting for us. Whilst he and Swallow discussed tactics I examined things for myself. The field rose steadily for fifty yards. Only then could we be seen by the enemy – providing no more 'nests' sprang up. This particular one must have been in residence when the second runner ran back over the ridge. The way they had ignored him marked them as a formidable crew. The

132

left side of the field levelled out on to the track – no hope of slipping them there. The right side dipped into a hollow bordered by a hedge. The ground on the far side of the hedge rose steeply. The Spandau crew would spot us at once. We had to chance the hollow. Swallow and the C.S.M. came to the same decision. Once again we set out, only this time there was no talking, and we were careful to keep the regulation five yards' distance between each man. As we moved across the hollow I kept one eye on the hedge, thirty yards to our right. It came to a corner at a point half-way across the hollow; one branch led back to the farm and gave cover from view, the other led towards the Spandau and offered nothing except a ditch. As we drew level with the corner the Spandau opened up again. This time he had us. There were no ridges. I raced Gibson for the corner of the hedge. He won. I flung myself into the ditch in front. To my horror I found it was only a few inches deep. The Spandau crew must see me. They could. They fired burst after burst from point-blank range – about eighty yards judging from the sound. Bullets hit the ground in front of my face. I jerked it into the ground.

'Gibson!' I shouted.

No answer.

'Gibson! For Christ's sake answer!'

He didn't. I cursed him. A bullet ricocheted off my foot. Another hit me in the calf. I felt the blood pouring down it. There was no pain. My heart hammered so fast I thought it would burst.

'Dear God!' I prayed. 'Don't let me die until I've had a woman!'

133

Wriggling out of my haversack I pulled it in front of my face. The Germans fired a single shot – a revolver bullet from the sound – which hit the haversack. I heard it coming. After that I played dead. It wasn't difficult. A mortar opened up on the field. Some shrapnel hit the hedge. I automatically presumed it to be German, although it could well have been one of ours. It made no difference to the Spandau crew. They gave me a burst every few minutes.

After what could have been anything between half an hour and an hour I heard a drumming of feet – from the direction of the enemy. They headed straight for me.

'They've come to finish me off!' I thought.

Looking up I saw Roberts. The Spandau didn't fire – until I got up. I ran a few yards and then dropped. Gibson's Tommy lay in the ditch beside me.

'He's buggered off!' I thought.

Jumping up again I raced for the farm. I had twenty yards to go. The Spandau fired the whole way. Roberts was hunched up by a doorway. At its foot was a culvert. I fell into it, deliberately. I was afraid if I jumped the Spandau – which was firing high – might have some luck. As I landed bullets crashed into the door. It sounded as if someone was throwing bricks at it.

'You all right?' said Roberts.

I nodded.

'They seem to like me,' I said.

We hammered at the door. Those inside took their time to answer – understandably enough, considering bullets were still whacking into it. Eventually an Italian opened up. He smiled at us like an indulgent father.

134

Boys will be boys. We tumbled inside. The first thing I did was to look at my leg. There wasn't a mark on it. The bullet had been a ricochet, the blood – sweat. My next thought was for Gibson. Had he really run? In the passage-way I met a medical orderly.

'Have you seen Gibson?' I asked him.

'Yes. He's badly wounded. In the head. He crawled in by himself.'

'I'll get those bastards!' I thought.

Turning to the Italian I pointed towards the field and said '*Fenestra?*'

'*Si, si!*' beamed the Italian.

He led me upstairs and into a bedroom. The shutters of the window were slightly ajar. I could see without being seen. But before I could stop him the Italian opened one shutter. He stood back proudly, as much as to say 'Look what a beautiful window I've found you!' The Spandau fired straight through it. The Italian kept very still, but his eyes rolled towards the bullets hitting the wall. When the Spandau stopped he quickly closed the shutter, and gave me another enormous smile. I sat down on the bed and rocked with laughter.

'What's going on?' shouted the C.S.M. from the bottom of the stairs.

I told him, adding that I thought the gun had moved up. I asked the Italian if there was another window. He shook his head. I went out to look round the sides of the house. On my way I found Swallow and the rest of the section sheltering in a cellar. I had no intention of waiting for the Spandau crew to find me there and said so. But the sides of the farm were depressingly exposed. Our only chance of nabbing the gun seemed to lie in catching him as he came round the farm. To do this we would have to find a position farther to the rear. I told Swallow I was going to look for one. It didn't take long to find a hedge from which we could cover the track-side of the farm. When I reported back to Swallow he asked if the other side was covered as well. I said I thought so. He sent me back to make sure. It was covered. The section set out for the hedge. We were almost there when the Spandau opened up. Swallow and the others dived for a gap in the hedge.

'Don't panic!' I shouted. 'They're not firing at us!'

For a moment I experienced the joy of being unafraid. Then bullets whipped past me. I dived for the gap – and stuck half-way. My pack had caught. The harder I shoved the firmer I was held. Bullets showered me with twigs.

'Give me a pull!' I screamed. 'Fire at them! Do something, for Christ's sake!'

No one did anything. There was only one thing left. I reversed, tore off my pack, then crashed through the hedge. On the other side I met the cook. He pointed down the hedge.

'There's a shed up there,' he said.

When we reached it I collapsed. Getting stuck in the hedge had finished me. I could think of nothing else except the Spandau. I was obsessed with the fear of it getting me.

Two Italians crawled into the shed carrying a flask of red wine. Whilst we drank they showered us with encouragement. It might have been half-time at a football match. I was amazed at such innocence. As they chattered on I had a sudden fear that the

Spandau was creeping up on us. Crawling out of the other side of the shed I found myself in a farmyard opening out on to the track. If I kept close to the hedge – which cut back to the track – I could see any-one who passed before they could see me. The gap's frontage – hedge on the right, farm on the left – was about thirty feet. I lay down and watched it. Like someone doing the pools I began working out all possible ways the Spandau might come – if the crew had tunnelled into the yard I don't think it would have surprised me. I soon found one for which I had no answer. Suppose they crossed the track near Com-pany rear H.Q., moved up under cover on the far side of the track, and then approached the gap going *up* the track, instead of down it? I wasn't going to get caught like that – oh no! I crawled down to the gap, keeping well over to the left, and looked as far round the corner as I dared. What I saw reassured me. The far side of the track sloped steeply into the valley – I had forgotten this – ruling out the attack I feared.

As I walked back up the yard some guns opened up from our lines. They had the peculiarly theatrical bang of 75 millimetres. That meant the tanks were behind us. Not far off judging by the sound. If I could get one interested we'd soon settle the Spandau. Telling Swallow what I had in mind I slipped round the back of the farm. There wasn't a tank in sight. Worse, the ground behind the farm rose steeply. The Spandau could hardly miss me running uphill. The tanks were shelling a village – it must have been Laterino – to the left of their forward squadron. The fire was concentrated on a church steeple, a favourite place for observation posts. One shell hit the bell, which clanged loudly. This amused me.

Returning to the yard I lay down by the hedge and listened to the Company's battle. The mortaring was continuous. The bursts of Spandau grew longer and longer. I sensed the desperation behind them. The Company must be putting in its attack. How many casualties would there be? The contrast between the Company and the section made me feel more ashamed than ever. But it would have taken more than shame to get a spark out of me.

I was still listening to the battle when I heard a carrier. It was coming down the track.

'Don't let it happen!' I prayed.

The Spandau opened fire. The sound went right through me. My body jerked like a hooked fish. But when the gun stopped the carrier was still moving. I watched the gap, horribly afraid of what I would see.

It wasn't a carrier, it was the Honey-tank. Bennett lay on its front, in a pool of fresh blood. Dead. The driver had his head low down. Slumped behind him like a frightened child, Cooper. The fourth member of the tank was standing up on one leg. Swathed from head to foot in bloody bandages he held his arms out like a cross. Just as the tank disappeared I realized why he was on one leg. His right foot was missing.

I kept staring at the gap. In my mind's eye the tank was still passing. It still is. What I had seen, and what I hadn't done. I felt sick with guilt. The blood was on our hands. And the look on Cooper's face. The Christ-like rifleman made it worse. A man with his foot blown off had had more guts than the whole section put together. The only thing left for us was to attack the Spandau. This, I knew, we would never do.

An hour before dusk the cook volunteered to run over to rear H.Q. He brought back the news that the Company had taken their objective and were going to withdraw. The section was to rendezvous with them at a farm near the river.

When we arrived there we found a Sherman parked outside. The crew were sitting in the kitchen.

'Hullo!' said their officer. 'You look as if you could do with a brew.'

We sat down without speaking.

'Here you are, chum,' said a trooper, giving me a cup of tea. It was strong and sweet.

'Our old man's been on the air,' said the officer. 'He's awfully pleased with your chaps. They've done jolly well. They're on their way back now.'

'One of your Honey's got Spandau-ed,' I said. 'It was our fault.'

'It happens to the best, don't worry. Have you heard the Division's being pulled out at Florence? I've got a bet with my driver we'll be there in ten days.'

'Money for old rope,' said the driver.

'Don't you believe it!'

I laughed. Then I remembered the Company.

'Which way are our chaps coming back, the track or the valley?'

'Track.'

I jumped up.

'The Spandau will get them!'

'I should think he's gone home by now,' said the officer. 'Sit down and have some more brew.'

I shook my head, and went outside. Head cocked I

listened for footsteps. Everything was quiet. I paced up and down the yard, haunted by the thought of another ambush. Then I heard a muffled tramping. I stared at the ground until the steps grew loud. Dashing back into the farm I said 'The Company's coming down the track, sir!'

The officer grinned.

'I told you he'd gone home.'

'Thanks awfully for the brew,' I said.

And for everything else.

When the Company arrived Swallow reported to Captain Kendall. The rest of us rejoined the Platoon. I slipped behind Humphreys.

'Everyone all right?' I asked him.

'Tomkins stepped on a Schu-mine. Titch and Mr. Simmonds wounded in the face. The Eyeties were leading us up a path. Don't step on the grass, they said, it's mined. Course Tommo 'as to go and step on the bastard. One of Five Platoon went to 'elp 'im, and 'e trod on one. Mr. Simmonds and Titch were running in be'ind 'im. Sammy got the blast. 'e's 'ad it now. That bloke in Five Platoon, 'e's got some guts. 'e 'ad one foot blown right off but as they took 'im away 'e shouted, "I'll be back, lads! I'll be back!" 'e and Sammy went back in the Honey. Mr. Simmonds and Titch walked through the valley. Some of Five Platoon with 'em. What 'appened to you?'

'Pinned down by a Spandau. Gibson got it in the head. What about the attack?'

'We had a real dabble! I used up eight Bren mags. First we cleaned 'em out of some 'ouses and they scarpered up the 'ill. Kendall says "Fix bayonets and charge the buggers!" We belted after 'em but they'd 'opped it. Then two Spandaus opened up from a ridge. Phil got one of them. A Ted jumped out of the pit and ran up shouting '*Wasser*! *Wasser*!' 'e was dead before we could give it 'im. The tanks got the other. One of their officers told them to surrender in German. They kept on firing until the tank went over 'em. Then the tank put its track in the pit. And they put a round of 75 in, too. Just to make sure. Good boys, the Lothians. Change from those other wallahs.'

That night I dreamt I was lying on top of a hill. I heard someone creeping through the undergrowth. It was an enormous German. I let him get close, then stood up and pulled the trigger. Nothing happened. My gun had jammed. I awoke in a sweat of terror. Telling myself it was only a dream I rolled over and went back to sleep. In the morning I felt fine. The previous day might never have happened.

'We're getting some smashing N.C.O.s!' O'Connor told me. 'Slim Wilson, Stan Towers, and Dick Saddler! I was on the Desert with 'em! They've been on the guns since Alamein – and they haven't used 'em since Tunis!'

'We'll miss Titch,' I said.

'Yerrah but I tell you we're lucky. You see.'

We passed Coke, sitting outside his bivouac. He gave us a huge 'I-told-you-so' grin.

'You'll get that grin wiped off your face, Cokey,' said O'Connor.

Coke sneered.

'Yerrah?' said O'Connor, and stepped towards him, fists clenched. But at that moment someone laughed. O'Connor swung round.

'There they are!' he said, pointing across the field.

'The three twins!'

The three N.C.O.s were walking towards us arm-in-arm. One look at them and I knew O'Connor was right.

'That's Slim in the middle!' he said.

Wilson had a smile that lit things up. I could feel it thirty yards away. He was also well over six foot. It was a striking combination.

'So they've tumbled you lot at last!' shouted O'Connor.

'Get away, you old bomb-slinger! We had our time in the Desert.'

'Yerrah? Just wait till you're running up and down these fucking hills!'

We all laughed.

'Which is Two Section?' asked Wilson.

O'Connor led him to it. Towers, a full corporal like Wilson, took over Phillips's section, and Saddler came to Swallow's as 2nd I.C. He was a handsome, rugged man just right for a Western. He made no attempt to hide his feelings about coming to the Platoon.

'We had our share on the Desert,' he said bluntly.

We rested for three days. I spent most of the time strolling round the harbour. I had no after-effects from my Spandauing. If anything I was the better soldier for it. I had always had the idea that because of its rate of fire – eleven hundred rounds a minute compared to the Bren's six hundred – one Spandau was worth two Brens. Now I realized that such a tremendous rate of fire must make the gun difficult to control, and really accurate shooting impossible. As a scatter-gun, at night, at long range, or for continuous fire – here the Spandau, belt-fed, scored heavily over the Bren – the Spandau was supreme. But for accuracy it was the Bren every time.

I envied Humphreys and the other sections their part in the battle. They'd had a taste of victory, as well as getting their own back in the way of bullets. The Spandau nest that had refused to surrender fascinated me. I tried to imagine the feelings of the crew.

One morning there was a sudden downpour. I dived underneath the nearest three-tonner. Captain Kendall was already there. He smiled.

'How are you getting on?' he asked.

'Oh, all right, sir,' I said, pleased at his interest.

He nodded.

'Yes, the Company's got its tail up now. They pulled themselves together very well the other day. We'll soon be a good one.'

I couldn't get over the fact that he had said this to *me*. But what could I say in return? As I groped for words the rain stopped. I scrambled away without saying anything.

The same day we had a N.A.A.F.I. issue that included a bottle of Guinness per man. Such abundance amazed us.

'Drink it quick,' said Humphreys. 'Before they ask for it back.'

But there was no mistake. The Company had simply indented for its nominal strength issue, when in fact it was down to nearly half that figure – Four Platoon were seventeen strong – and it happened to be a 'wet' one.

Three Section, reinforced for the occasion by O'Connor, made an opening of it. Saddler – Swallow had left us for Six Platoon – demanded silence.

'Tops off!' he shouted.

We toasted everything we could think of. But when we drank the grins faded. The Guinness was sour. Our yells of disappointment stopped some Italians in their tracks.

'Might as well give it to them,' said Saddler disgustedly.

We walked over and offered one of them a swig.

'*Buono!*' he said excitedly. '*Multo buono!*'

Within a few minutes we had swopped the Guinness for a demi-john of wine. This softened the blow.

On the third day of the rest Wilson – Meadows was acting Platoon Commander – called the Platoon together.

'The Company's going on a big recce tomorrow,' he said. 'If we bump the enemy we fuck off.'

The 'O' group was over. We had had our first experience of the Wilson touch, and we liked it.

The Company was dressing for the patrol when a strange three-tonner drove into the field. A military policeman stepped out.

'They've come for Cokey!' shouted O'Connor.

'About time!' said Humphreys. 'You'll be there, Cokey!'

Coke didn't say anything. He just grinned and packed his kit. We watched him climb into the back of the truck. Once there he turned on us.

'You silly sods!' he yelled. 'I 'ope you don't get pulled out at Florence!'

This shook us. For a moment no one answered him. Then Humphreys shouted 'And we 'ope you'll be fucking shot!'

The truck began moving.

'I'll be alive when you're all fucking dead!' shouted Coke.

We shook our fists and yelled, but although none of us would ever have admitted it I think we were all a little impressed. Coke had gone down with all guns firing.

The Company moved off, quickly shedding Rifleman Roberts who suddenly told Saddler he wasn't going any farther. Wilson's section picked up a couple of deserters near a village called Corsaro. The rest of us passed through the village, waved on excitedly by the inhabitants – they had enough savvy to stay indoors. The enemy were obviously very near – and Five Platoon soon bumped them. The Company then withdrew through the village. I won't forget the look on the faces of the Italians who watched the liberators depart.

'Bit rough on them, isn't it?' I said.

Saddler nodded.

'Clever stuff, this patrol.'

Half an hour later, when Four Platoon had set up a road-block a mile away from the village – the rest of the Company had marched back to the harbour – a group of frenzied partisans ran up the road. One who spoke French told me that the previous night the Germans had hidden a pile of ammunition in Corsaro. Once we had passed through the village the inhabitants had handed it over to the partisans. As soon as we had left the village the Germans had re-entered it. When they found their ammunition missing they had begun to beat up anyone they could lay hands on. When were we going to attack, asked the partisans? They could show us a safe way in. I had to tell them we weren't going to attack at all. The partisans blew their tops and left. Not long afterwards another group appeared. Would we lend them some Tommies? We didn't dare take the risk. Meadows indicated that they might have better luck with the crew of a Sherman tank who were parked behind us – tank Q.M.s were renowned for being blind-eyed about missing equipment. The crew of the Sherman dished up three Tommies. The partisans cheered. They then squabbled furiously for the weapons, watched by us and their leader, who was wearing a sword and looked like Ramon Navarro. The lucky partisans threw away their rifles, their leader got them into file and then, to our astonished delight, drew his sword. '*Avanti*!' he shouted. Off they went. As they reached a bend in the road they began singing. It was heroic. It was also comic-opera. We didn't know whether to laugh or cheer. As they disappeared round the bend a Spandau opened up. The partisans reappeared at the double, shouting like mad and throwing their weapons into a ditch, and vanished into a maize field. That did it. The Platoon howled with laughter. For some reason I accompanied my own laughter by hitting the ground with my fists and I went on till they were sore.

We'd hardly calmed down when we heard a motor-bike coming up the road from the harbour as if his life depended on how quickly he reached us. The cyclist tore into our fork of the crossroads and pulled up inches short of our road-block – a tree trunk. The rider was a sergeant in the Military Police. We stared at him in amazement. He stared back furiously and then, having made sure there was no officer present, he let fly.

'Get that bleeding tree out of the way, will you!' he roared. 'I'm due in Corsaro at six!'

For a moment no one said a word. If ever there were seventeen men with a single thought it was then. Should we let the bastard go? Meadows looked round at us and then shrugged.

'Yes, Sergeant,' he said softly. 'We'll move the tree. But I suppose you know Corsaro is still occupied by the enemy?'

I'll say this for the red-cap – he moved. He was away like a Grand Prix ace. But not before he had heard our jeers. He'd remember us.

Our relief was due at eight. They arrived at midnight. When we got back to the harbour Captain Kendall met us.

'Sorry about that,' he said. 'There's a hot meal waiting for you.'

This news didn't have its usual effect on me. I collected some stew but when I tried to eat it my stomach heaved. You've been eating too many melons, I thought (I had eaten five during the recce).

That night I dreamt that flies were crawling in my mouth. I woke and they were. I had a horrible taste in my mouth and it had nothing to do with flies.

It was breakfast-time. After a few spoonfuls of porridge I had acute diarrhoea. I didn't have time to reach the latrine. It's only gippy-tummy, I told myself. But I had never felt ill with gippy-tummy. And the stool was bloody. On my way back to the section's area I had to dive back to the latrine. I soon realized it was pointless to leave it. When anyone else

147

came along I took to the bushes.

I finally left it at lunch-time. O'Connor ran up to me.

'What's up?' he said.

'Gippy-tummy.'

'Coo, you look terrible! You're for the M.O. Slim! Come and help me take Alec sick!'

'The M.O.'ll say I'm swinging the lead,' I told them.

'No he won't!' said O'Connor.

After asking what was wrong and taking my temperature the M.O. scribbled something on a card and hung it round my neck. A signaller drove me to the Divisional Dressing Station. On the way I looked at the card. 'Stretcher-case – suspect dysentery.' That sounded real enough.

The Divisional Hospital was miles behind the Line. But when we arrived I caught an unmistakable whiff of cordite. The orderlies who helped me out of the Jeep were jumpy.

'We just been shelled!' said one of them. 'Big stuff! We was queueing up for dinner. There was a fucking great whistle and the biggest bang you ever 'eard. I fell on top of Bert. When we gets up there was no dinner. No cooks neither. Mixed up with the meat and vegetables they were. Poor old Nobby – 'e was our cook corporal – we found 'is 'and. We knew it was 'is 'cos Nobby bit 'is nails.'

At this point I'd had enough and asked what hospital he thought I'd go to.

'Arezzo, I should think. Under canvas.'

He took my temperature, and then began to fuss me with pillows and blankets. When he'd gone I looked at my chart. My temperature was 103°. I had nothing more to worry about – unless the Germans decided to try their luck again. It amused me to compare the hazards of a Divisional Hospital with those of the Company's harbour.

Within the hour I was on my way to Arezzo. I spent the night in a transit hospital. I had a room, and eighty-four outsize pills, to myself. An orderly woke me up every two hours to hand me the pills. In the morning I felt much better. When I arrived at Arezzo two Italian orderlies tried to put me on a stretcher. I waved them aside.

'I'm O.K.,' I said. 'I can walk.'

Feeling rather heroic I reported to a medical orderly sitting beside an M.O. He took my case-card and after copying the particulars passed it on to the M.O. The officer glanced at it, then looked at me.

'What's wrong with you?' he said with a sneer. 'A touch of diarrhoea?'

Only fear of the 'glasshouse' stopped me hitting him. The look on my face made the M.O. drop his eyes.

'All right! All right!' said the orderly hastily. 'You go on in there!'

I walked into a large tent containing a dozen beds, one of them empty. An English nurse greeted me pleasantly and led me to the empty bed. Once between the sheets, and with the nurse out of the tent, I let my neighbours know what I thought of the M.O. I then felt like a smoke. When I went to take the pipe out of my pocket I found the stem was missing. This upset me more than the M.O. had done. The nurse came in to find me almost in tears. She quickly rustled up a spare stem – a straight one – and fixed me a 'short-arsed Charlie'. It looked odd but it worked.

9
THE CARDINAL'S HOUSE

I spent five days in hospital. It was good to lie
between sheets and do nothing except gossip. The
man next to me was from the 1st. The King had just
inspected his Battalion.

'They pulled us out of the Line,' he said, 'and made
us scrub our equipment. You know what it was like
when we left Egypt? It was like that, only whiter.
God knows how long it'll take to get khaki again –
the Teds'll see us for miles.* Anyhow, they fell us in
on a road and along comes the old King. The tank
blokes gave him a big cheer – *their* equipment was
the usual dirt-yellow. When he comes to us the officers
shout "Hip-hip-hooray!" – all by themselves. I felt
sorry for the King. It wasn't his fault. It was that twat
of a general.'

From hospital I went to a convalescent camp. On
my first walk I saw a patch of water-melons. I helped
myself. It seemed unlikely I would be unlucky twice
running.

Two days later I was on my way up the Line. My

---

* At Taranto we had blancoed our equipment every day for a fortnight. Only then had it become khaki coloured. Whitish equipment
worn over a camouflage smock was the sort of target a sniper dreamt
of.

travelling companion, a signaller from Divisional Headquarters, presented me with a pipe – my own was really not worth the trouble.

'A Guardsman gave it to me,' he said. 'He took it off a Ted from the Hermann Goering Div.'

The mouthpiece had been bitten through, but the pipe's associations made up for that.

The transit-camp where we spent the night was one in a thousand. Instead of the usual dirty blankets and bad food we had clean blankets and food that would have done credit to a good hotel. The queue for dinner went on for hours. Most men had two helpings, and some of us had three. It was the same at breakfast. There was bacon and egg – real egg, something I hadn't seen since Egypt. I was remarking on this to the signaller when I came face to face with a rifleman from 'D' Company.

'How's the Company?' I asked him anxiously. 'Have Four Platoon had any casualties?'

'They're all right, but Captain Kendall's dead.'

It was like someone hitting me over the heart.

'The Company had just got in a village,' continued the rifleman. 'And the Teds were stonking us. One of the carriers came up. Captain Kendall went out to talk to its commander, and a shell landed right next to him. He died before they could pick him up.'

The rifleman went on to talk about his own hard times, and how the M.O. had sent him back with 'battle-fatigue'. He seemed quite proud of this. But I was glad to have him natter on. It gave me something to hang on to, and I began to think as well as feel. The Company had lost its greatest commander, and with him its one chance of being great. Of that I

152

was sure. And I had lost something else, something I couldn't put into words. Whatever it was I knew it would be hard to replace. I also knew it would be fatal to brood about it. As the rifleman described a battle prior to the one in which Captain Kendall had been killed I made myself listen to the details, and the shock wore off.

After lunch, when the sun was directly overhead, and everyone had retired for a siesta, there was a sudden stir. I looked out of my bivouac and saw men running towards a field that bordered the camp. Those already there were lined along it like fans at a football match. A sudden cheer confirmed the obvious. They were watching some sort of sport. But who was crazy enough to perform in such heat?

When I got there I saw that the 'teams' consisted of a dozen military police and three German prisoners. The Germans were gazing at the sun. As I tried to grasp what was happening one of the prisoners dropped his head. A red-cap punched it up again. The crowd cheered.

'What's going on?' I asked the man next to me.

'The Teds shot their escort. On their way to a P.O.W. cage. They won't say which one of 'em did it.'

'Scorching their eye-balls out, they are!' said his mate.

They both laughed. I left them to it.

I caught up with the Company the following evening. They were queueing up for dinner. As I joined them Corporal Bailey walked up to me.

'It's good to have you back,' he said.

I blushed with pleasure. It was the greatest compliment I've ever had, and it still is.

Then O'Connor saw me. Putting his hand in his pocket he pulled out my missing pipe-stem.

'Yerrah!' he chuckled. 'You dropped it in the signals Jeep. You're a lucky man, you are. But you've missed some fun! Coo! We've got a new officer – you should see him!'

'Slim!' he shouted. 'Come and tell Alec about Sally!'

The three of us sat down on the grass.

'We had a pretty dodgy time mopping up some Spandaus,' said Wilson. 'When we came out for a rest – we thought – we got this officer. The next thing we heard the Company was attacking a village. The lads got niggly. "When are we having a rest?" they said. So I went to have a chat with the officer. "Excuse me, sir," I said. "The men are up. They've had eight days solid in the Line. Can you tell us when we're coming out?" "The men are up, Corporal!" he says. "Up! Good God! When I was at Salerno we had three weeks in the Line! Up indeed. Don't let me hear any more of that sort of talk, Corporal!" So I went back to the lads and warned 'em we got a proper M.C. wallah for an officer.'

'Tell him about the village!' urged O'Connor.

'We drove into it, instead of marching. Captain Kendall's idea.'

'Yerrah, he got those men killed!'

'We got mortared on the way. Two blokes in Six Platoon copped it. When we got in the village—'

'Let me tell this bit, Slim!' interrupted O'Connor. 'Yerrah, the Platoon got into a *casa*. Stan Tower's section were upstairs. A new bloke called Burroughs had the Bren. When Stan opens the window a Spandau

154

fires straight in. "Fire the Bren, Burroughs!" shouts Stan. Nothing happens. Stan turns round. No Burroughs. "Where the hell's he gone?" says Stan. "Under the bed," says Page. And there he was, wrapped round the Bren like a bint. "Give us the bloody thing!" says Stan. But he wouldn't let go of it. Stan had to kick his fingers. And whilst he's doing it Page picks up Stan's Tommy, sits down with his back to the window, and fires it over his shoulder! Yerrah, someone should make a play of it!'

O'Connor seized up with laughter, and Wilson took over.

'The Spandau fucked off, but a bit later a Patrol turned up. You couldn't miss 'em. We did, though. Too excited. "A poor show, Corporal," says the officer. "A very poor show." After that things were quiet. Me and Dick got our feet under the table with the Eyeties who owned the *casa*. They were bloody good to us. Brought out the old vino and cooked us a chicken. We were all getting down to it when in walks the officer. "Ah, Corporal," he says, "Chicken." "That's right, sir. Chicken." He waits for a bit, and when he sees it isn't coming he says, "Could I – um – have a bit, Corporal?" I gave him the parson's nose. "Thank you, Corporal," he says. "Thank you very much." And out he walks. "The bloody scrounger!" says Dick. The next minute Page shouts, "There's a Ted coming down the road!" We ran out of the room and bumped into the officer. "Corporal!" he says, "I'm going to fire the Piat!* No one's to fire until I do! Is that understood?" He grabs the Piat and fixed it up on a landing half-way up the stairs. I got back to the section's window. The Ted was marching slap

155

down the middle of the road. He was an officer – dressed up like a dog's dinner. There was a bloody great bang from the Piat and then we all had a go. The old Ted dived behind a wall – you've never seen anyone so *jildi*! We stopped firing. Dick says, "They won't send *us* to Bisley." Then we heard a moaning noise from inside somewhere. I ran on to the landing. The officer was lying at the bottom of the stairs – the Piat was in two bits, half-way down. The thing had knocked him flying. "Are you all right, sir?" I asked. He just goes on moaning, so I hopped down and helped him up. After he'd felt himself all over he turns to me and says, "Oh, Corporal, I'm up!" Then he hoves off into the kitchen. Dick looks at me and says, "When I was at Salerno! Let's call him Sally!"'

Major Dunkerley was once again Company Commander. O'Connor thought this was great.

'We're well rid of Kendall,' he said.

'You wouldn't say that if you'd seen him in action,' I told him.

'He got those men killed,' repeated O'Connor stubbornly. 'The Company should never have driven into the village.'

He had me there. To make an approach-march by three-tonner seemed to be asking for trouble. If the Company had gone in on foot they might have made the village without being spotted. On the other hand Kendall's main object – to inject the Company with his own aggressive spirit – must have been on his

Fn to p.155. * Projector, infantry, anti-tank. An effective if alarming weapon – the first time I had fired it the barrel had 'gone off' with the bomb – built on the lines of the early cross-bows. If held loosely its recoil could break a man's collar-bone.

mind when he laid on the mobile attack. Perhaps his experiences in the Recce Corps had prompted him to use trucks.

I was sorry to have missed the fun. And the shooting. This time I was more worried than envious. When was I going to fire back?

That night I was woken up by returning revellers. Phillips was carrying a live goose, someone else had a hen under each arm, and bringing up the rear were three riflemen, two ducks, a cock and nine young turkeys.

'We've had a smashin' time!' said Phillips. 'First we had some vino and then we met some of those tank wallahs. The bastards let us down again so we got stuck into 'em. It was a lovely fight!'

It was a lovely goose, too. We had it for lunch the next day. And when we left harbour we took our livestock with us. We now had something to rival Five Platoon's piano.

I have a soft spot for ducks and had just started to pet them when an explosion rocked the truck. Once we had recovered from the shock – the blast had hit us badly – we looked out and saw a gun-crew. Their grins made it clear that they had deliberately held their fire until we were passing. If the convoy had stopped we would have half killed them. As it was we just yelled and shook our fists. The gunners enjoyed this.

When we settled down again I looked round to see how the menagerie had taken the blast. The cock was as arrogant, the hens as stupid, the turkeys as motherless, as ever. But the ducks' eyes were glazed with terror. Delighted with their intelligence I did my best to comfort them.

A few hundred yards farther on we left the road. As we got off the trucks the enemy gunners opened up. The heavier-than-usual shells made a curious 'wobble-wobble' noise as they passed overhead. We were leisurely digging ourselves in when one of them fell short. The old cry 'Stretcher-bearer! Stretcher-bearer!' echoed across the field. But the wounded man, the Company pay-clerk, died before they reached him. Everyone had liked him, except those after his job.* He was too young for it, they'd said (he had had his nineteenth birthday earlier in the month), it should have gone to an older man. O'Connor, who was particularly fond of him, was with him when he died.

'There won't be any more talk about his having a cushy job!' he said bitterly.

The Company moved to another harbour. In the morning a lance-corporal and two riflemen from Five Platoon went out fruit-picking. We heard a big explosion and presumed it was sappers blowing up mines. In fact it was Five Platoon picking fruit. The party had entered an orchard smothered in white tape and cross-boned notices saying 'Keep out! Mines!' They had taken off their berets to start picking when a Sapper Major saw them from a Jeep. He told his driver to pull up. As he stood up to order them out of the orchard one of the riflemen picked a plum. Half the orchard went up. The two riflemen and the Sapper Major were killed outright, the lance-corporal severely wounded. The driver remained to tell the tale.

* Pay-clerks did not go into action.

One of the riflemen had left a wife and six children. Someone passed the hat round for them. And someone else, inevitably, drew the moral: 'They asked for it, didn't they?' It was a toss-up whether the lance-corporal would avoid a court-martial. If he did it would be because of his injuries.

The evening 'O' group produced a major surprise. The Company were to spend the night in billets. We could scarcely believe our ears. Phillips smelled a rat.

'They got something in store for us,' he said. 'You see.'

In a way he was right. Four Platoon split themselves up in a roadside farm and I shared a double bed with Saddler – and bed-bugs. The bugs didn't touch Saddler. They bit me alive, much to Saddler's amusement. In the end I got out of bed and slept on the floor.

On the outskirts of the nearest village, called Regello, there was a large house. The Platoon had to find out if it was still occupied by the enemy.

An hour before setting out the section received a replacement. Saddler and I took one look at him, then whispered 'Watch your kit!'

On reaching the house we found the Germans had left the previous evening. Blessing our luck we moved into the servants' block – the house itself, an enormous mansion, was locked and bolted. Saddler, the replacement and I had a room to ourselves. There was no electric light so Saddler made a lamp by filling a cigarette tin with petrol, and stubbing flannelette through a hole in the lid. I was helping Saddler move equipment when something made me look round. The replacement had the lamp in his hand. Before I could say a word he pulled the lid off. A 'boomph!' of flame shot across the room. All the walls caught fire. Beating at the flames with our hands, Saddler and I yelled curses at the replacement who stood there, lamp in hand, looking like something out of shock-headed Peter, and telling us he had 'only tried to make it work better'. The fluency of our cursing helped us douse the fire. In the morning Meadows handed on the replacement to one of the other platoons.

The 1st were occupying some houses a few miles the other side of the village. The Company was to relieve them. When we had carried out a tour of patrols we would probably have a rest. The fifteen-hundredweights were to accompany the Platoons, a good sign.

The route to the Platoon's house took us through the sort of wood Dante reserved for suicides. The trees on either side of the track had been strangled by mould-ridden creepers. These hung over the track like snakes. The stench of the rotting trees reminded me of the dead. The croak of bull-frogs – the three-tonner was doing its best to sound like a Rolls, and the frogs almost drowned the engine – provided the appropriate noises off. After a few breezy comments on the creepers we found the atmosphere a bit too much for us. We sat and listened to the frogs.

"ere, you blokes,' said Humphreys suddenly. 'Any of you see that film with Boris Karloff? "The 'aunted 'ouse?"'

The changeover took place in pitch darkness. I could make nothing of the house, except that it was big. A rifleman led Saddler into a room on the first floor. It had two windows. Sullivan and the Bren took the bigger. I was to relieve him there. In the event of a stand-to I was to man the other window. Saddler took over a window on the landing. This left me two hours to enjoy a double bed. It was a beauty, and I soon sank into the same state of trance as I had experienced during the night attack. When I heard Page shout 'Halt!' and call a password I took in what it probably meant but part of me refused to function. It was too comfortable. Page fired his rifle. Still I lay on the bed, unafraid. A Spandau opened up. The burst hit Sullivan's window, and a bullet struck the wall above my head. It was like the petrol going 'Boomph!', except it was fear instead of fuel. Rolling off the bed I crawled over to my window. Sullivan was firing the Bren. I picked up a grenade and looked through a hole in the shutter. I couldn't see a thing. I looked at my knees instead. They were shaking like twin-motors. I looked through the shutter. This time I could see the ground. It seemed a surprisingly long way away. (In the morning I discovered that my window overlooked a much lower courtyard than the one we had entered by.) Then I saw a black shape. As I stared at it it began moving. I grabbed the pin on the grenade – and then had second thoughts. I shut my eyes. When I opened them again, the shape had stopped moving, and I recognized it for what it was – a bush.

Saddler padded into the room.

'I think they've buggered off,' he whispered.

We stood-to for another hour, and then I took over Sullivan's post. When I came off guard it was breakfast-time. As soon as we'd eaten Saddler told the pair of us that Sally had ordered the section to find out where the Spandau had fired from. Empty cartridge-cases would give us the clue.

The house was in a hollow. As we climbed a bank overlooking Sullivan's window we could see the whole building. It was a modern villa about eighty yards long and twenty-five broad. I remarked on the oddity of the shape.

'It's a cardinal's place,' said Saddler. 'His summer residence.'

We found the cartridges on top of the bank. As we were examining them we heard someone behind us. We swung round – and saw a peasant with his horse and plough. He waved to us. We waved back, and watched him work his way over a ridge.

'Spandaus don't worry him,' said Saddler.

I nodded. It seemed almost too good to be true. Here was a man setting about his daily bread as if the war was a cloud in the sky. I felt awe and a tremendous sense of affirmation.

When we returned to the house I had a look round. The 1st might have missed something. I worked my way from room to room without finding so much as a handkerchief. The last room led into a smaller one. This contained a chest and a cupboard. The chest was full of junk, the cupboard 'sheeted' with brown paper. I walked away in disgust. Then I had a thought. Why was the brown paper so spotless? Why wasn't it dusty, like the stuff in the chest? I went back and pulled aside the paper. What I saw took my breath away. Hanging there, like the plumage of some magnificent bird, was a silk cloak – white silk embroidered with crimson and cloth of gold.

162

'I can't take that,' I thought. 'It's out of my class.'

On a shelf at the top of the cupboard I found a cap made of the same material as the cloak. That was more like it. I stuffed it in my pocket, along with two corks with silver tops.

I returned to the section's room in triumph – and found O'Connor there to share it with.

'Look what I've found, Paddy!' I said excitedly.

O'Connor looked as stunned as I must have done when I saw the cloak.

'Coo!' he said. 'You can't take them, Alec! That's the cap the Cardinal wears when he gives communion! And those are the corks for the holy wine!'

'Good Lord,' I said. 'I didn't know that.'

'Better put them back, Alec. It's unlucky to take holy things.'

I had no intention of putting them back.

'No,' I said. 'I didn't know what they were when I took them. I'm hanging on to them.'

O'Connor laughed and shook his head at me.

'You're a deadly man, you are!'

The more I thought of the cloak the more I wanted it. I had never had such a lust. Bad luck or not I was going to have it. But as I walked down the corridor an Italian emerged from the room, and locked it after him. He was swearing horribly. I ducked out of sight. When the coast was clear I returned to the section. It was probably just as well. If I had pinched the cloak the Italians would probably have complained to Sally. And I still had the cap. It would make a lovely night-cap for my mother.*

* She made a lampshade out of it.

163

There were a number of spare mattresses around and I used them to 'sandbag' the front window of the section's room. I enjoyed myself. It isn't every day one has a chance to play gangsters. Saddler came in as I was applying the finishing touches.

'What are you at?' he said.

'Keeping out the old Spandau.'

Saddler looked impressed. I wasn't quite such a twot as he'd thought.

'We got company,' he said. 'Couple of partisans. Bullshitting about patrols.'

I went down to have a look at them. They were giving a demonstration.

'*Tedeschi li*!' said one of them, pointing across the table.

'*Partigiani*, burr-burr, burr!' said the other swivelling his sub-machine-gun round the table.

'*Tedeschi finiti*!' shouted the first one.

'The winning goal,' I thought.

I envied them their attitude, but not their job. It was bad enough fighting a war with each side taking prisoners. To fight one knowing you'd almost certainly be shot or tortured if captured was that much worse. It was easy to blame the Germans for shooting partisans. But vice versa! Partisans can't afford to take prisoners – food and manpower are too precious. The fact that both Germans and partisans sometimes broke the no-prisoner rule is the thing to wonder at.

Later that afternoon Major Dunkerley phoned up Sally and gave him a warning. The partisans had reported that the enemy were sending us a fighting patrol. They could be expected any time after dusk.

At nine o'clock Battalion H.Q. rang through to say

that all regimental patrols were in. There were no other Allied units in the area. Anyone approaching the house would be enemy. We were to dispense with the password for the day, and shoot on sight.

The Platoon stood-to until one o'clock. Those not on guard then went to bed. I was one of them. I didn't fancy a repetition of the previous night and determined to keep wide awake. But the bed proved too much for me.

I woke up knowing someone was near me. It was Saddler.

'They're coming down the drive!' he whispered. 'We can get them from the landing!'

I got up. My throat had gone dry. When I picked up my Tommy it seemed to have doubled in weight. Would I have strength to fire it?

Saddler was on the landing, cradling the Bren.

'Don't fire till I drop my hand,' he whispered. 'Then we'll get the lot.'

They were coming down the drive, all right. 'Crunch-crunch-crunch!' went the boots. It sounded like half the German Army. What a way to patrol. But then the Germans always did make a lot of noise at night, or so I'd heard. It gave them 'Dutch' courage. I could have used some myself. Would I be able to pull that trigger? You've always been on about getting your own back, I thought, well now's your bloody chance. But this wasn't how I'd imagined it. This was going to be a massacre. The screams of the dying, retaliation from the living – I was terrified of both. Only doubts about trigger-pulling kept the horror at bay. I could see them now. A formless mass, thirty yards away. Saddler raised his hand. The faces showed white. Fifteen yards. Saddler dropped his hand. I took first pressure on the trigger. It gave.

'Is that "D" Company?' said an unmistakably regimental voice. 'This is "C" Company here. We got a bit lost.'

Saddler must have answered him. All I remember is dropping on to the bed, and shaking from head to toe. When the fit passed I had only one thought – to get my hands on whoever had told us that 'all our patrols are in'.

Next morning Saddler got on to Sally about it. Sally said 'the matter was under investigation ' (that was the last we heard of it). He then told Saddler that he was to take a reinforced section on a patrol. Then I was called in. All the Platoon's N.C.O.s were there and they were grinning. Sally was not.

'Your section is going on patrol,' he said. 'There is only one map and I – ah – need that myself.' I took this to mean 'There's a good chance of the Patrol not coming back so I'm going to hang on to the map.'

'I want you to draw another one,' he continued.

'Right, sir.'

Sally gave me the map. Once out of the room I began laughing. Every year at my prep school we had to draw a chart showing the line-up of the Battle of Trafalgar. And every year my chart looked like an action painting of the actual battle itself.

Saddler joined me in the corridor.

'Fuck the section's luck!' I said.

We laughed out loud.

The object of the patrol was to reconnoitre a particular hill. The enemy was known to be on either side of it. If the hill was unoccupied I was to mark everything we saw from the top of it.

As I copied the original I noticed it was dated 1913, and wondered if anything had changed in the years.

The section's reinforcements consisted of Page, Booth and a newcomer called Groves, whom I recognized as the second runner at Laterino. We set out after lunch. For the first mile all went well. Then we came to a track. Beyond it lay a hill. This was as it should be. But on my map – and this part tallied with the original – the path we were on continued on the other side of the track. In fact, the path ended at the track. Noticing that the hill had a lot of young trees on it I told Saddler I thought the path must have been overgrown. He nodded.

'We'll go up in file,' he said. 'Fifteen yards between 'em.'

I led the left column, Groves the right. There were too many shrubs around for my liking. We could easily be ambushed. My eyes swung left, swung right – and saw Groves looking up at the sky. He was carrying his rifle as if it was a shopping-basket. This frightened me almost as much as the idea of an ambush.

'You've been dumped,' I thought.

After this I watched Groves's frontage as well as my own.

The higher up the hill the thicker grew the trees. We'd been climbing for a good half-hour, and I had just given us up for lost, when we struck a clearing. Through the trees on one side we could see a valley, and in it a river, and several houses. I consulted my map.

'You know, Dick,' I said. 'According to me we're a

mile behind the German lines.'

Everyone laughed except Groves.

'Mark in the *casas*,' said Saddler. 'We'll see what we'll do afterwards.'

Using my knee as a table I began marking. The pencil kept on going through the paper.

'Alec's marking in the shell-'oles!' crowed Page.

Down in the valley there was a sudden and startling burst of singing.

'Teds 'aving a piss-up,' suggested Page.

'Partisans more like it,' said Saddler.

'I think it's the "International",' I said. 'Perhaps the Teds have packed it in and chummed up with the Eyeties.'

We stood there relishing the idea. Then, with a suddenness as startling as the singing, I sensed something wrong. In the clearing. I looked round. The trees walled us in. No one could creep up on us. And yet.

'You know, Dick,' I said. 'There's something fishy about this place.'

Saddler nodded. This surprised me. I had expected a 'Come off it!'

'Finish the map,' he said. 'And we'll scarper.'

A minute later Saddler drew us up in single file. I was tail-end Charlie. As we moved off I felt someone looking at me. I swung round, finger on the trigger. Nothing but trees.

'You're getting windy,' I thought.

I'd gone another five yards when there was a 'whoosh!' A mortar-bomb burst on top of us. We threw ourselves into a gully. As more bombs crashed down Groves jumped up and ran down the hill.

'Don't panic!' yelled Saddler.

He kept running. It was touch and go whether I joined him. Only a strong sense of shame stopped me. The enemy were now fairly pasting the wood. They must have thought they were breaking up an attack.

'O.K.,' said Saddler. 'We'll shove off now.'

He led us down the gully at a dignified pace.

'We must have been on top of them,' I said.

Saddler nodded.

'Listening post. Waited till we were clear. Bubbly bastard!' he added, pointing at a distant glimpse of Groves.

I kept quiet on that one. We collected Groves at the bottom of the hill. Saddler bollocked him mercilessly but he didn't seem to mind.

Sally was delighted with our bump. For some reason drawing the enemy's fire rated as a splendid piece of work. My map, which now looked like a dirty paper handkerchief, ended up at Company H.Q.

The partisans reported that the enemy patrolled the track at the bottom of the hill every night. Sally decided to send the whole Platoon out on an ambush patrol.

We duly laid up along the track, but the partisans got in first. As I listened to the fight I thanked God I wasn't a German. One enemy was quite enough.

Next morning the Platoon carried out three more patrols, Saddler's section exploring a farm encased with German signal wire. Leaving Sullivan with the Bren Saddler and I followed it up on hands and knees, going in opposite directions. We met at a corner.

After lunch we went back again. As we neared the farm Saddler hissed at us to get down.

'There's a Ted!' he whispered. 'Working on the wire!'

Sullivan saw him at once. I didn't. Saddler tried to point him out.

'He's there. By the tree. In a camouflage suit!' he whispered.

I still couldn't see him. But what I could see was that the ground between us and the farm was wide open. A covering Spandau would get the lot of us. Saddler must have had the same idea.

'We're on a recce,' he said. 'Good enough to say we spotted this bloke.'

Sally sent Wilson out with a fighting patrol but when we got there the bird had flown.

The night passed quietly. First light found me on guard.

'They won't come now,' I thought, and leaning on the table on which I had placed the mattresses I fell fast asleep.

Someone shook me gently. I jumped with shock. It was Meadows.

'It's all right,' he said with a smile, as I began making excuses. 'I've come round because Sal said something about inspecting the sentries to see if they were on their toes. I got in first. Luckily. All five of you were asleep. Not surprising, either. We could do with some.'

News that the 5th were relieving us came through at breakfast. Satisfied with our score-card Sally dropped all patrols, and the Platoon slept.

10
BLESS RELAXES

On its return the Company moved into the mansion proper. The Platoon had a suite on the ground floor. There were beds a-plenty but no loot. An expedition upstairs righted this. The raiders returned laden with silk stockings and women's underwear. Page had a night-dress, and Humphreys began 'seducing' him. O'Connor dropped in to see the fun.

'Yerrah!' he said. 'It's lucky this *casa* belongs to a Fascist!'*

I went to go upstairs myself but Sullivan stopped me.

'You've had it,' he said. 'Five Platoon's got the bedrooms. They kicked us out.'

I persuaded him to part with a silk-and-suède cushion embroidered with a horse's head and sprinkled with gold dust. Humphreys gave me a garish pink-and-white silk shirt – a 'conscience money' gift, I'm sure – which I wrapped round my Tommy. I made up for a late start in the library. The books were all in French and Italian, and it seemed piggish to

* O'Connor had the rather convincing idea that all landowners must have supported Mussolini. This particular one turned up later in the week. Far from complaining about our depredations he did his best to treat us like guests.

take them for their binding. Instead I chose an ivory-and-silver snuff-box and a paper-bound song-book entitled *British Army Songs*.* This consisted of some twenty World War I songs analysed by German World War II propagandists. The only song I had heard sung, or had sung myself, was:

> 'I don't want to join the Army,
>   I don't want to go to war,
> I'd sooner hang around,
>   Piccadilly underground,
> Living on the earnings of a high-born lady.'

'This', wrote the commentator, 'shows that the Tommy's heart is not in the war. He would prefer to be at home.'

Although Regello was still part of the Line the sector could hardly be called a fighting one. We did have one scare though. The night after the Germans had sent a patrol into the village – the partisans ambushed them, and killed one man – two of the Company's sentries vanished. Their rifles were lying in the courtyard, and it looked very much as if they had been taken prisoner. In fact they had deserted, and were picked up a few weeks later on the Arezzo-Rome road.

C.S.M. drill-parades were a feature of our first week at Regello. These took place on the road leading to the village. The road was still under observation by the enemy, a fact that did not pass without comment. We were more amused than anything else.

---

* This, my most treasured souvenir, went the same way – the very same way, I suspect – as my Florence trousers.

Only a mob like ours, we decided, could drill in front of the enemy.

One evening I strolled down to the house where Saddler and I had shared a bed. As I turned a corner I bumped into a crowd of village girls. They took one look at me and shrieked with laughter.

'*Pipone!*' they shouted. '*Pipone! Pipone!*'

For a moment I thought I had scored a mass-conquest. Then I realized it was my pipe. The girls fluttered around like humming-birds. I grabbed at the sexiest one but she darted out of range. I took my pipe out of my mouth, but it made no difference. The damage was done. I was the visiting clown. Exasperated by their laughter I charged them. They all escaped except one who didn't try to. She was shy and very young, not at all what I wanted. But something about her eyes, and the way she used them, held me. They were velvet-soft, like a fawn's. We stood around awkwardly without speaking. In the end she told me her name was Violetta, and we arranged to meet the next evening.

When I arrived I found the whole family – father, mother and sister – waiting for me on a balcony. They were very friendly and I was soon telling them all about my adventures in the Cardinal's house (I left out the one about the cap). Violetta's mother chimed in with '*Poveri Soldati cosi lontano dalle madri!*' It was nice to hear this again. The family then withdrew. Violetta and I sat cheek-to-cheek and watched the sunset. I never dreamt that such slight physical contact could have such an effect. I could have sat there for ever.

The next day Violetta and I walked out with her

sister and another rifleman. The rifleman soon steered the sister into the bushes. I tried the same on Violetta. She took her arm away. The Good God would not approve, she said gravely. I had no answer to this, and didn't really want one. Violetta was enchanting enough as she was.

One evening I had just sat down with the family when Violetta said '*Guardi!*', and pointed at my trousers. I looked down and saw I had just two fly-buttons left. Violetta ran indoors. I went scarlet. The family laughed, and told me not to worry. Violetta would fix it. She returned with a sewing-basket. Before I could say a word she began sewing on buttons. For a moment I longed for the earth to open. But the family looked on as if the sewing happened every day. I lost my embarrassment, and realized how absurd some conventions were.

During the Company's second week at Regello the Germans cleared off completely. The village held a memorial service for two partisans. O'Connor and I attended. The partisans trooped in armed to the teeth – one of them was carrying a bazooka – and when they sprang to attention it sounded as if they were wearing armour. I had to stifle a grin. But once the village priest got going it was another story. At the end of the sermon the whole congregation was in tears, and so was he. Neither O'Connor nor I had understood a word except '*Il buon Dio*' but that hadn't made any difference. We both needed handkerchiefs.

By now the whole Battalion was resting. The following day Saddler and I were on Company Office.

'I'd like to make you a Company sniper, Bowlby,'

said Major Dunkerley. 'Will you accept the post?'

If he had said 'I'd like you to take over the Company' I couldn't have been more surprised.

'Yessir,' I said automatically.

Once out of earshot I burst out laughing. Poor Major Dunkerley! If only he had known my capacity for not seeing Germans, let alone shooting them. Saddler had also been made a sniper, but then he was a natural. Nevertheless I took the job seriously. During a stalking practice – in an olive grove – I crawled to within five yards of Page before he spotted me. The same day I went out for a private shoot with my Tommy. Although I would be using a special rifle for sniping, I felt it would do no harm to have some automatic practice. Besides the idea of a sniper with a Tommy amused me. Sitting on one side of a stream I let fly at a tree on the opposite bank. A woman screamed. For a terrible moment I thought I'd hit her. How, I couldn't imagine. The bullets had struck the tree. A ricochet? The place where the screams were coming from, beyond the top of the bank – which was thirty feet high – made this impossible. Even ricochets don't go round corners. As the screams continued I realized they were hysterical. I had frightened myself almost as much as I had frightened the woman, and left in a hurry.

A companion piece to this happened during a morning's Piat training. The Company had been issued with a new type of bomb that had a highly sensitive nose-cap. The slightest knock would set it off. When we arrived at the 'range' – a desolate stretch of landscape guaranteed clear of civilians – Meadows decided to make sure the Piat was in good working order before we tested the new bomb. With the rest of us standing just behind him the Piat-man fired six 'old' bombs without any trouble. Then, using the Piat as a mortar (it made a much better one than the Platoon's two-inch) he tried some new ones. The bombs worked beautifully. To round things off he tried a 'straight' shot at a tree. When he pulled the trigger the bomb moved gently out of the barrel, and dropped towards the ground beneath it. The bomb's tail-fins jammed in the muzzle. Its nose hung an inch from the ground. For a second or so nobody moved. Then Meadows stepped forward and removed the bomb.

'All right, lads,' he said. 'That's enough for today.'

Three days later the Company held a dance. I had never been much good at dancing and took a skinful of Marsala to help me on my way. Unfortunately I overdid it and was sick. I then went to sleep. When I woke up it was getting dark. I went back to the dance and found Violetta sitting by herself. She cut short my apologies. It didn't matter at all, she said. It obviously had mattered, but she was too sweet-natured to show this. As we walked down to her house together she told me that the Company was moving very soon, probably the next day. Civilians always seemed to know more about our movements than we did ourselves but the suddenness of this surprised me. There had been none of the warning signs. 'You will come back,' she said to me, and I said yes, I would.

Violetta's 'grapevine' was accurate. Immediately after breakfast there was a buzz of 'O' groups. The

Company was pulling out at four o'clock that afternoon. By ten o'clock the courtyard was like a market-place – stores being loaded, weapons cleaned, runners running, and N.C.O.s shouting. The arrival of a batch of replacements added to the confusion. They were a most unlikely-looking crowd.

'They're ack-ack wallahs,' said Meadows.

'They look like it!' said Saddler.

He pointed to an effeminate-looking private with blond hair.

'They brought Goldilocks with them!'

Goldilocks and five others reported to Meadows. Humphreys approached Goldilocks with a big smile.

'Welcome to Four Platoon,' he said. 'We 'ope you'll be very 'appy with us.'

Goldilocks looked pleased.

'How nice of you to think of saying that!' he said in a mincing voice.

'Oh, we're all nice 'ere,' said Page, who had sidled up behind Humphreys.

'You look as if you were an artist or somefink,' said Humphreys.

Goldilocks blushed.

'Yes, you're quite right,' he said. 'In civvy-street I was a tap-dancer.'

'No!' said Humphreys, a wicked gleam in his eye.

'Yes,' said Goldilocks. 'I play the piano, too. It was ever so nice in my last unit. All my friends watched me practise.'

Humphreys rubbed his hands.

'Well, well, well! You couldn't 'ave chosen a better

Platoon. We're *all* musical 'ere. My friend Page plays the violin smashing, don't you, Charlie?'

Page looked suitably modest. Goldilocks stared at him.

'Do you really?' he said.

'Course 'e does!' said Humphreys harshly. 'I gut the cat for the strings!'

It was like pulling a switch. The Platoon howled with laughter. Goldilocks burst into tears.

'You horrid beasts!' he shouted. 'If I had my friends here they'd show you! They'd show you!'

This made Humphreys clutch hold of Page for support.

Meadows put an arm round Goldilocks.

'You mustn't mind them,' he said. 'They're only taking the piss.'

Three replacements, all Welshmen, came to Saddler's section. But it was no longer his section. O'Connor, of course, heard the news first.

' "Judge" Jeffreys is coming to the Platoon!' he said. 'He's a lovely man, is Judge! Do you know he was on the Desert three years and I never heard him complain, not once? He'll take over your section, Alec – you're lucky!'

'Well, I'm shoving off to Slim's section as soon as he comes,' said Saddler.

I was wondering what I would make of Jeffreys when Swallow paid me a visit. He showed me a letter from Gibson. G. would soon be invalided out of the Army. He had been hit just as he had thrown himself down by the 'safe' part of the hedge, the part I had tried so hard to reach myself. The bullet had gone through his forehead, destroyed his right

178

eye, come out through his jaw, and ended up in his chest. He was partly paralysed and couldn't eat properly. The letter, which was remarkably cheerful, made me think a bit.

The mail also included a carton of two thousand cigarettes for a signaller who had been killed at Perugia. The cigarettes were shared out amongst the Platoons. It was a brutal yet poignant reminder that you can't take it with you.

Corporal Jeffreys arrived just before we moved off.* He was a big, worried-looking man who looked curiously out of place in uniform. I imagined him wandering round a farm, fearing the worst.

The whole of Regello turned out to see us off. As we approached Violetta's house I looked out and saw her and her family. I waved. They waved back. Then Violetta burst into tears.

'What you done to 'er, Alec?' said Humphreys.

'Leave him alone,' said Jeffreys. 'We'll be back, don't worry,' he said to me.

I kept very quiet. I was horrified to find that the thought of leaving Violetta didn't worry me in the least.

The Company's move had coincided with the fall of Florence. We were heading for a sector some fifteen miles east of the city. We reached our destination – a farm eight miles behind the Line – soon after dark. Jeffrey's section had a loft to themselves. I got one of the three beds. This brought me in contact with a Welshman called Morgan. He looked as

* And Phillips went to Company H.Q. as N.C.O. in charge of transport maintenance.

179

if he had just been dug up. And he spluttered as he talked. When he saw me putting my kit on the bed he got very excited.

'That's my bed, man!' he said. 'I saw it first!'

'You should have put your kit on it.'

'I tell you it's my bed man, man!'

It looked as if I would have to fight for it, but then another Welshman came to my aid.

'You've had it Morgan, boy,' he said, and winked at me.

Owen, as he was called, guided a protesting Morgan to the other end of the attic. Then Jeffreys arrived back from an 'O' group. The first thing he did was to take deficiencies.

'Are you short of anything?' he asked me.

'Emergency ration.'

Jeffreys looked at me earnestly.

'Are you sure you've lost it?' he said.

That wasn't playing the game.

'Yes,' I said guiltily.

Jeffreys looked so worried that his conscience pricked mine. I wished I'd said 'No', and then, angry at this, nearly said, 'You're not paying for it.'

'Anything else?' said Jeffreys.

I shook my head. I knew that whilst Jeffreys was in charge of the section I would never indent for 'lost' kit.

After breakfast the next morning some twenty-five-pounders had a shoot. I was stripped to the waist, sluicing my face, when an explosion sent shrapnel flying past me. I flung myself on the ground. It was surprising how much more vulnerable I felt naked. I presumed we were being mortared but

180

in less than a minute – the speed with which such news got round always surprised me – the 'grapevine' reported that a twenty-five-pounder had had a shell explode in the breech. One of the crew had been killed.

During the night the enemy had ambushed a fighting patrol from 'C' Company. Out of fifteen men four, including the officer had been killed, three wounded, and four were missing. As soon as it was dark Four Platoon was to send a fighting patrol to the same place – by the same route. This staggered us.

'What about laying on a brass-band?' said Humphreys. 'Case they don't 'ear us coming?'

The R.A.F. had photographed the area. We examined the result. Everything looked beautifully clear. Jeffreys was pointing out the route to the section when Saddler walked over.

'You're only seven strong, aren't you?' he said.

'Yes,' said Jeffreys suspiciously.

'We're nine. How about having one of ours?' Jeffreys smiled. I was astonished by the change in him. The lines in his face burnt themselves out. In place of the worry was a most endearing self-depreciation, a 'what does it really matter?'

'All right,' he said. 'I'll buy it.'

'He's let you in,' I told him.

'Do you think so?'

It was Goldilocks, of course.

After lunch the Company went to bed. When we dressed for the patrol I put on my Desert boots. Their crêpe soles would be useful on a patrol.

As soon as it was dark we drove to our respective start-lines. The Platoon's turned out to be on the edge of a wood. Sally picked me as leading scout. The thought of my Desert boots cushioned the blow. At least they wouldn't *hear* me coming.

Our route lay through the wood. As I passed Sally he grinned.

'It's all right, Bowlby,' he said. 'They never shoot the leading scout.'

I grinned back. It wasn't bad for Sal.

Fifty yards inside the wood I came to a churchyard. It seemed an odd place for one. Then I noticed something odder. The yard was strewn with freshly broken branches. There was something fishy about that. As I nosed my way across the yard some guns fired. The shells screamed towards the church. I flung myself into a culvert running alongside it. The shells crashed down. Some hit the church. The interval between the guns firing and the shells landing was exactly two seconds. That put the guns – 88s by the sound of them – very close. For a nasty moment I thought the Germans had got wind of us. How I couldn't think. Then I remembered the branches. When the barrage lifted the yard had a lot more of them.

Jeffreys crept out of the darkness.

'Are you all right?' he asked anxiously.

'Yes. Good start, isn't it? They're right on top of us.'

Jeffreys nodded.

'No one hurt,' he said. 'But Groves buggered off as soon as the shelling started.'

I remembered Groves day-dreaming on the Cardinal's hill. Clearly it was better to have too much imagination than too little.

Just beyond the yard I had another surprise. Lying across the road was the biggest tree I'd ever seen. It was like looking at a six-foot wall topped with a fence of branches. In front of it stood a bulldozer. The enemy had blocked the track and were doing their best to see it stayed that way. I looked hopefully at the sides of the road. They were ten feet high, and sheer. We had to climb the tree.

'Just the place for a booby-trap,' I thought, eyeing the tightly-packed branches.

Page, my number two, gave me a shoulder, and I pulled myself up. Half a mind on booby-traps I tried squeezing my way through the branches. It was like pushing a locked gate. I would have to break my way in. This I did. The noise frightened me, until I got caught between two saplings and forgot about anything else. The harder I struggled the more firmly I was held. I threshed around wildly until one of the saplings broke with a resounding crack. I stood listening for the 88s. They must have heard that. Nothing happened, so I scrambled through the rest of the branches – and saw another tree stretched across the road.

There were eight all told. It took an hour to pass them. By then the moon was up. It was full. Once clear of the wood I saw the road spiralling into a valley – and my own shadow cast before me like an uninvited guest. It went round the bends of the road before I did. The enemy would see it before I saw them. And behind me Page's army-issue boots went 'clippity-clop!' like the old Grey Mare herself. So much for my Desert boots. At each bend I flicked forward the Tommy's safety-catch. I stopped dead at one. The windows of a house stared straight at me. The door looked like a mouth – a witch's mouth. Two hundred yards of road between us, but the house covered the lot. Just the spot for an ambush. I waited for Jeffreys to catch up with me.

'If there's anyone inside they'll have us taped,' I whispered. 'What about slipping behind the hedge?'

'Hang on. I'll ask Sal.'

Jeffreys came back looking upset.

'It's not on, Alec. He says we've got to keep to the wood.'

'The cunt!'

Keeping my eyes on the window, my finger round the trigger, I bore down on the house. The nearer I got the more certain I became that it was occupied. The enemy were holding their fire, as Saddler and I had at the Cardinal's place. What surprised me was my certainty that I would fire back. Where this resolution came from I didn't know, but it was there.

A hedge covered the house. As I crept into the drive I tripped over a wire. I fell heavily, my mind jerking with horror. Trip wire. S-mine.

'Are you all right, Alec?' said Jeffreys.

He put an arm round me. I'd never felt so safe in all my life.

'Yes, I'm O.K. I thought it was a trip-wire.' We grinned at one another. Jeffreys helped me up, and we examined the wire.

'It's signal stuff,' said Jeffreys. 'Ted. We'd better follow it up.'

'Yes, I suppose we should.'

To my relief Jeffreys decided to search the house first. But the door was locked and the windows shuttered. We crept round it like a couple of burglars. Wilson met us in the drive.

'We're searching some *casas* over the road,' he said. 'Sal wants you to stay put till we're finished.'

'Let's have a look at that wire,' said Jeffreys.

We traced it round the house, and half-way down a hedge. Jeffreys seemed in two minds whether we should follow it up, or wait for Sally. As he hesitated the 88s opened up. The shells howled past the house. We crawled back to the section, who were bunched up on a bank near the road. This faced straight on to the 88s. Providing the shells continued to land beyond the house we were safe. But shells passing a few feet over one's backside give one a nasty feeling.

'Why can't we go in the house, man?' hissed Morgan.

'It's locked,' said Jeffreys.

'We can break it open!'

'It would make too much noise.'

'Too much noise, man! With all these bloody shells!'

I had to bite my lip to stop myself laughing out loud.

Jeffreys crawled over to Morgan.

'Look,' he said. 'The section is staying here. Do you understand?'

Morgan kept quiet – until a shell dropped just the other side of the bank. Then he got to his knees.

'I'm not staying here to be fucking killed!' he said.

'The Welsh are windy buggers,' observed Sullivan.

'Windy!' said Morgan. 'It's common sense, man!'

Sullivan didn't bother to answer. Morgan muttered to himself and lay down again. Soon after this the guns stopped firing. I couldn't quite make up my mind whether they had been after us or not. I was still wondering when an engine started up. It was the bulldozer. The 88s opened up before the driver could get his second rev. in. They fired flat out for ten minutes. This time nothing dropped within a hundred yards of us.

In the silence that followed the barrage Morgan began hearing noises.

'There's someone behind the house!' he whispered.

We all listened.

'Can you hear anything, Alec?' whispered Jeffreys.

'No.'

Goldilocks began whimpering.

'It's all right,' said Jeffreys. 'There's nothing to be afraid of.'

I was beginning to feel nervous myself.

'Shall we have a look round to make sure?' I said to Jeffreys.

'Good idea.'

First we crept round the house. There was nobody there. Then we searched an orchard. Apart from cordite fumes nothing was out of place. Finally we combed the ground in front of the section. I was no longer nervous. Facing a danger, and finding it doesn't exist, gives one a lift. I stepped on to the section's bank – and found myself looking into the muzzle of Morgan's rifle. He was trying to pull the trigger, but his hands were trembling too much to do it. I took this in at once. For a good second I stood there enjoying his terror. Then, articulating each word as if teaching English to a foreigner, I said, 'Put that fucking thing down!'

The satisfaction I got from saying this still warms my heart.

At the time I had another source – the 88s of all things. They and the trees had interfered with the patrol's schedule so much that I knew there must be a good chance of us not going any farther. Nor, in fact, did we. There remained one last surprise. Down in the valley a bird began singing. At once I remembered the Perugian 'cuckoos'. Were the gunners signalling to a patrol, sent to sniff us out? But as the bird sang on I realized that no human could reproduce such perfection. It was a nightingale. And as if showing us and the Germans that there were better things to do it opened up until the whole valley rang with song. Once again I sensed a tremendous affirmation that 'this would go on', only this time the wonder of it overwhelmed me. I could only lie there and let it pour in.

When the nightingale stopped singing Sally told us to pack up. Back at the churchyard we got the unmistakable 'feel' of trouble. A white-faced Swallow spotted me.

'We've had three men killed!' he said. 'We were in the tower. A shell came right through the wall. They got the driver of the bulldozer as well.'

And the Germans had also ambushed the Company's other patrol, severely wounding a Desert-booted officer and two riflemen.

When I woke up next morning Jeffreys and O'Connor were sitting by my bed like two doctors with a favourite patient. Jeffrey's eyes had so much affection in them that I could only look back at him, half mesmerized.

The Company were queueing up for a combined breakfast-lunch when eleven Thunderbolts flew over. They were low enough for us to see the American star.

''ow many planes in a squadron?' asked Humphreys. 'Twelve, ain't there?'

'Eleven,' said Page.

'Twelve!' said Saddler.

'Garn!' said Page.

A moment later a twelfth Thunderbolt appeared, flying at the same height, and in the same direction.

'Told you,' said Saddler.

The plane went into a power-dive and headed straight for us.

''aving a bit of fun,' said Humphreys.

With an appalling 'pom-pom-pom!' the plane opened up with its cannon-guns. The queue vanished. It was like a conjurer waving a wand. Shells crashed into the farm. The plane straightened out, gained height, then came down again. This time it was after the twenty-five-pounders. When he'd shot them up twice he went after something else a mile or so away. Then, having presumably run out of shells, he flew off after his squadron.

The gunners reported two guns damaged but no casualties. One of our tank-regiments had lost a tank, two of its crew being killed. In their usual casual way the powers-that-be never bothered to let us know if the pilot was brought to book.

That night all three Platoons went out on standing patrols. Jeffreys' section had a tank leaguer to guard. Why couldn't they look after themselves, we demanded. Weren't they big enough? They had been out all day on patrols, we were told.

188

Once the section was under way – we had a three-tonner to ourselves – the Welsh began singing. Owen had a fine tenor but the other two were almost as good. Morgan the unutterable became Morgan the bard. He growled away in a rusty bass that would have roused the Men of Harlech. Owen rounded off the 'traditionals' with something of his own.

'I've got to get to Heaven on an old push-bike,
    The wheels are rusty, and the brakes don't work!'

I forget the rest, but the song never did a better job. We arrived at the leaguer in high spirits. But the tanks were revving-up. That seemed all wrong. The sound would carry for miles. Whilst an officer explained the details of the guard to Jeffreys I asked a trooper what all the noise was about. Maintenance, he said. The officer led us to the side of the leaguer that faced the enemy. Jeffreys posted Owen at one end of the hundred-yard long leaguer and me at the other.

'Bombhead' Rogers popped out of a house behind me to ask where Jeffreys was. He had to shout to make himself heard. The engines roared on. I wondered why the enemy didn't shell us (the leaguer was only half a mile from the bulldozer church). Perhaps the 88s had pulled out. Either that, or they were sending us a bazooka patrol. They'd know where to come.

One by one the tanks quietened down. The last gave a five-minute solo. This brought me to screaming point. So much so that I forgot to take into account what the effect might be when the tank stopped revving. This proved costly. The silence, the suddenness of it, unnerved me. I'd got bazookas on the brain. I

189

knew they'd come. Up a hedge. That was it. A covered approach, snaking up from no-man's-land. And sure enough I saw a line of men moving up it. With a horrible fluttering of the heart I just stood and watched. It was lucky I did. It gave me time to notice that although the men were moving they weren't getting any nearer. I shut my eyes. When I opened them again the 'men' had gone.

'Get a grip,' I muttered.

But how? In a flash I remembered the words of an English master at school. 'Many men in times of sorrow and stress have found comfort in a few lines of verse,' he had said. It was worth trying. The line

'What passing bells for these who die as cattle?'

came into my head as if it had been waiting its cue. And I could not shake it off. In desperation I recited the rest of the sonnet. This caused a wave of depression and self-pity. I was still in it when Sullivan relieved me.

My mood sent me to sleep. A bomb, whistling into the valley, woke me up. The plane was heading our way, flying low. When it was just above us it dropped two flares. Night turned into day. Goldilocks got up and ran. Jeffreys and I collared him.

'You mustn't move,' said Jeffreys quietly. 'Or they'll see us. Do you understand?'

'Yes,' piped Goldilocks – Jeffreys was sitting on his back, and I was on his legs. The plane dropped another flare. I waited for a bomb. But when the flare died out the plane flew off towards our lines. The three of us walked back to the section. I had just made myself comfortable when the plane headed in our direction – and opened up with its cannon-guns. A shrieking whistle came straight for me. I clutched my head. The shell landed just behind it. The shock lifted me clean off the ground. When I looked at the 'shell' I saw it was only an empty casing.

An hour later a ground-fight broke out a mile or so to our left. The machine-gunning went on for ten minutes, and I counted over sixty grenades. The Germans had sent someone a fighting patrol. They were not likely to send us one as well. Nor did they.

The next morning the Platoon received a local leave vacancy. Four men, including O'Connor, had an equal right to it. O'Connor assured me he would get it and by the way he was chuckling I guessed he would. He did.

'Yerrah, I told Major Dunkerley I wanted to see the Pope!'

Twenty-four hours later the Company moved to another sector.

11
THE GOTHIC

This time the Platoon had a house to itself. The luxury palled when we heard we were to help sappers to clear a booby-trapped village. Some men in a three-tonner had stopped there to pick up a piano lying in the main square. When they tried it out they blew themselves to bits. The Germans had stuffed it with Teller mines. Other novelties included joints of meat strung with Tellers and S-mines in the lavatories.

The next morning the expedition was cancelled. Meadows cut in on our murmurs of relief by ordering Groves, Goldilocks and another of the newcomers to get their small-kit.

'You're to report to the M.O.,' he told them. 'He's sending you down the Line to be medically examined – to see if you're fit for front-line service.'

The three men fell out sheepishly and Meadows dismissed the rest of us. We were too dazed to move – until Wilson jumped out in front.

'Come on, me beauty – that's a good girl!' he shouted, catching hold of nothing. 'Come on my old grey mare!'

Saddler leapt behind him and began talking to a 'dog'. Page fed a 'baby'. Wilson mimed so well that his imaginary horse became as real to us as he was himself. We all ended up sitting on the ground, weak with laughter.

In the afternoon the Company took to the road again. We met Battalion rear H.Q. coming the other way. Fast. Their drivers had seen their first shell since Tunis.

'Where's the fire, mate?' we shouted. 'Where's the fire?'

That night we occupied a hill without opposition. Some long and alarmingly loud bursts of Spandau had us worried until Jackson compared notes with the other platoons and found that the guns were much farther away than they sounded – the hill's acoustics were to blame – and were firing on fixed lines. (The German habit of blazing away at night was a bad one. It showed us where the guns were and gave their owners a false sense of security.)

After I'd dug myself in I stood guard, then went to sleep. I woke up on my own accord. The air was heavy with moisture and I sensed we were in for a storm. Jumping out of my trench I warned the Platoon to unwrap their gas-capes. I had just unwrapped my own when the storm broke. The rain was torrential, the thunder and lightning fit for the gods. 'Blow, winds, and crack your cheeks! Rage! Blow! You cataracts and hurricanoes!' said I, snug beneath my gas-cape – I had jammed it over me, like a tent, avoiding condensation, and keeping the rain off everything except my boots – 'Spout till you have drench'd our steeples, drown'd the cocks!'

As if to show nature they knew a thing or two as well our gunners in the valley opened up with a divisional stonk. It was impossible to tell the difference between gun-flash and lightning, gun-fire and thunder. I enjoyed the show as much as I enjoyed peering through my gas-cape at the pool of water forming over my stomach. It was a good six inches deep when I decided to get my boots under cover as well. All it needed was a few careful wriggles. I duly made them. As I grunted with satisfaction the cape collapsed. The shock of the water hitting my stomach made me yell. The state it reduced me to – I was soaked to the skin – kept me at it. Jeffreys ran over to see what was wrong. By then I had begun to laugh. There was nothing else left to do.

The Ruffina sector – named after a small town in the valley – turned out to be almost as quiet as the Regello one. The Indians on our right put in an attack the day after we arrived. We didn't hear if it was successful. The same day Wilson took a patrol to a village on the hill adjoining the Company's. Finding it deserted he laid an ambush. A German sergeant and five men walked straight into it. They were too surprised to put up a fight. Later another German turned up to find out what had happened to the missing men, and Wilson put him in the bag as well. At about the same time as this was happening Jeffreys' section were on O.P. work on a ridge near the farm. There wasn't much to see but I took care to look round cover, and not over it. The C.S.M. arrived on a tour of inspection.

'Being a bit careful, aren't you?' he said.

'Not particularly.'

To show me how it was done the C.S.M. climbed up the ridge and looked over the top. Two shells skimmed the ridge. The C.S.M. slithered down it, losing his beret on the way.

That night an enemy patrol cut through a gap between us and the Indians, and shot up an Indian H.Q. The Indians suspected that the Germans had used a path that passed within half a mile of our farm. Four Platoon were to lay on an ambush in case they tried the same thing twice.

Whilst the patrol was being planned the Company had another batch of replacements. Four of the five who came to the Platoon belonged to the Regiment – they had been combed out of base jobs – and they brought some interesting news. Bates and Cross, the Platoon's Capuan deserters, were in hospital near Naples. They had been looting a house in a 1943 battle area, and one of them had trodden on a mine. The irony fascinated me. The fifth replacement, a Scot, came to Jeffreys's section. As soon as he saw Morgan he said: 'So you're here, you Welsh sod!'

Morgan replied in kind. Jeffreys had to step in between them. Owen told me that they had met, and fought, in a transit-camp. Five minutes before the patrol set out they were at it again.

The Germans weren't silly enough to use the same route twice and Four Platoon's ambush patrol passed without incident, at least that's how it would have been recorded at Battalion H.Q. In fact the patrol was one long series of 'keep-the-pot-boiling' quarrels – a continuation of Morgan versus the Scot, and then Morgan versus Sullivan. As soon as Jeffreys quieted one pair the other started up. Jeffreys became desperate. 'I can't do a thing with them!' he whispered. I was half-amused, half-sympathetic.

'Tell them the Teds are coming,' I suggested.

'I've tried that already!'

In the end the cold put an end to the quarrelling. We were still wearing light-weight khaki-drill. Major Dunkerley had already asked the Q.M. for greatcoats and had been told that they were on their way up from Taranto, along with the rest of our winter kit.

We had tomatoes for breakfast. We had had them two or three times a day for the previous fortnight. I was sick of the sight of them.

'Not again!' I groaned.

The cooks – all four of them – looked at me as if I'd sworn in church.

After breakfast Meadows told me the C.S.M. wanted to see me.

'My God! Is it about those bloody tomatoes?'

Meadows laughed.

I told him that if 'Bombhead' tried to come the old acid he'd get more than he bargained for. I was furious.

'The cooks have told me that you've made a complaint about the cooking,' said the C.S.M. quietly.

I explained that I had not made a complaint, it was just that I was fed up with tomatoes, and had said so.

'I quite understand,' said the C.S.M., in a voice of sweet reasonableness, 'but you must realize that the cooks do a great job of work. They're up all hours, and whilst you're resting they do the guards. You've hurt their feelings. I want you to go and apologize.'

I swallowed hard, and said I would. The thought of apologizing riled me but 'Bombhead' had left no way out.

The cooks accepted my explanations with frozen dignity.

'We didn't expect it from *you*, Alec,' said the cook corporal.

This made me crosser than ever. I had to stop myself really hurting his feelings. Instead I sought out a very amused O'Connor, who promised to try and put some sense into their heads.

During the afternoon the Scot disappeared. We never saw him again. Morgan was jubilant. That night's ambush patrol turned out to be as harmless and much quieter than the previous one. A fighting patrol from one of the other platoons reported that the enemy had pulled out of the village beyond the one where Wilson had taken the prisoners. The next night the drivers and the cooks – bless their tiny hearts – mounted guard whilst the rest of the Company slept in.

Two days later we moved to a rest-house in Ruffina. We were only twenty miles from Florence, and the drivers ran a 'bus-service' into the city. I must have been the only man in the Company who didn't use it. Like the sailors who were afraid to sail too far lest they fell over the edge of the world I was afraid of straying too far away from the Company. From where it was based. Since Perugia I had grown less dependent on individuals but, paradoxically enough, more dependent on the Company. It had given me the only real sense of security I had ever had. I was determined not to miss a minute of it. Instead of sight-seeing in Florence I sat under an olive-tree, watching the countryside, and chatting with the peasants.

One morning we had a visit from the Divisional Intelligence Officer. With the help of a large-scale map he showed us how the General had worked out a plan for cracking our sector of the Gothic Line. It was to be a tank show. The infantry would have a supporting role. Once the 'door' was open the tanks would swan through into the Lombardy Plain, and the Division would split the German Army in two. The I.O., who really did seem intelligent, made it all sound most convincing but I couldn't help thinking that tanks couldn't climb mountains, at least not the sort we were coming up against. There had been too much dark brown on the map for my liking.

The same day the Platoon heard it was to spend four days guarding O.P. officers on a mountain over-looking one sector of the Gothic Line. We would be the only Platoon from the Brigade in one Line. Our comments can be imagined. That night all four Welshmen came back drunk. Meredith, who was in Wilson's section, picked a fight with Morgan (Mere-dith had managed to fight someone each of the five nights we'd been resting). Owen separated them, and then swayed towards his blankets. They had the wall on one side of them, my own blankets inches from them on the other. I prepared to be trodden on but Owen avoided me. Once inside his blankets he began retching. He had the choice of being sick over me, or inside his own blankets. He chose the blankets. Manners maketh man.

After a three-hour drive through some very rugged country we left the three tonner and began climbing. It took the rest of the day to reach the top. In places the track was spiked with boulders. Having to pull oneself over them made a change from slogging but Page, Humphreys and I had gippy-tummy and were in no shape for rock-climbing. We soon dropped behind the others. As I rounded a corner I met a platoon of Guardsmen. Their page-boy officer glared at me fiercely. Their sergeant, a waxed-moustached male nurse, did the same. Two pairs of eyes shouted, 'Why aren't you with the rest of your Platoon!' The men grinned – they may have guessed what was wrong – and I grinned back.

Jeffreys was waiting for me at the top of the mountain.

'I told Sal you had gippy-tummy,' he said.

When the other two had caught up we walked over the flat until we reached a farm. I went straight to bed.

In the morning I saw that the farm was surrounded by two or three acres of maize. The idea of crops growing on top of a mountain intrigued me. So did the flatness of its summit.

When Wilson got ready to take his section on a recce Meredith refused to go. He knew he would be killed if he did, he told Wilson.

'I'm not forcing him,' said Wilson. 'He'd only leave us in the shit.'

When the patrol had left Jeffreys took the section off to the O.P. The officer we were to guard held the V.C. for observing under fire. Our presence would surely be superfluous.

The way to the O.P. lay through a chestnut wood. We were just too early for the nuts. The sound of a vehicle cut short our disappointment. How could anything have driven up that track? It was a Jeep, with two men and the biggest wireless set I've ever seen.

Once out of the wood we had another surprise. The view was fantastic. Mile after mile of jagged mountains, the nearest a razor-backed monster with pinnacles like Milan Cathedral's. The Gothic Line. No wonder the Germans had called it that. If their defences matched the mountains we might as well call it a day.

The O.P. officer welcomed us pleasantly. After we'd had a good look at his V.C. ribbon we sat down and listened to the Jeep's wireless. When they'd done the usual 'Roger out' stuff the signallers switched over to the B.B.C. 'Music while you work' came over loud and clear.

Wilson's patrol spotted an enemy convoy moving along a road not under observation. Next morning Sally took Wilson and Saddler to the same area. Wilson told me what happened.

'When we got near the place Sal sticks his head over a bank. A Ted took a pot at him. Sal moved back sharpish. "Get that sniper, Saddler!" he says. "Get him your fucking self!" says Dick. Sally goes pink. Then he looks at me and says, "Perhaps we should go home, Corporal." And I says, "Yes, I think we should." '

The next morning we heard that the Guards were attacking Monte Peschiena – the mountain opposite the O.P. When we arrived at the O.P. we heard firing and presumed that the Guards had bumped. In fact it was an exploding ammunition Jeep, stuck half-way along a road that joined the two mountains. The O.P. officer told us the Germans were having a map shoot – the valley road was not under direct observation, but the enemy could tell from dust-clouds when it was being used, and had their guns trained on the road. Their aim was uncannily accurate, he added. We saw this for ourselves. Another Jeep ran the gauntlet and the enemy shelled two stretches of the road. The shells that didn't score a direct hit landed close enough to slice anything using that part of it. The exploding ammunition Jeep provided an additional hazard. Heart in mouth I watched the live Jeep hare past it. Seconds later the Jeep was safely out of sight. Three dispatch-riders followed, at intervals of ten minutes. Then a three-tonner. On the last stretch it got a direct hit. The crew baled out. Shortly afterwards the derelict Jeep blew up with a roar.

Next day the Platoon joined the rest of the Company at the foot of the O.P. mountain. O'Connor greeted me with a bunch of muscatels. They served as a sweetener. The Company was taking over from the Guards now nearing the summit of Peschiena. Peschiena, some four thousand feet high, was shaped like a wedge of cheese. We were to approach it the 'long' way, and would have a march of over fourteen miles. The enemy consisted of two or three companies of Turcomen, luckless wretches who had been captured on the Russian front and had chosen to fight rather than rot in prison camps. The Guards had found six of them asleep round a Spandau, and one of a number of deserters told interrogating officers that the Battalion were living on blackberries. This was the sort of opposition we liked.

The Platoon had been reinforced by Groves. The medical board had grounded Goldilocks and the other misfit. They considered Groves a 'fighting man'. It was a pity they hadn't seen him in action.

Groves's arrival made the Platoon overstrength. We could at last afford the luxury of an L.O.B.* The choice narrowed down to Sullivan and myself. We drew cards. I won.

The Company were driving to the foot of Peschiena. The road was under fire and we were to go through at 50 m.p.h. Only when we were actually bumping over its shell-scarred surface did I realize we were crossing the 'mad mile' I had watched from the O.P. mountain. This shook me. Half-way across the convoy halted. Goaded by the crash of shells I blew my top. I told the Platoon exactly where we were. Nobody put me in my place. As soon as the shelling lifted we shot forward again. The enemy gunners 'blanketed' the road. The three-tonner was repeatedly hit by shrapnel and the windscreen splintered but we got through.

Whilst the bulk of the Company set off up Peschiena rear H.Q. moved into a farm two hundred yards from the road. I was between the two, enjoying the idea of being L.O.B., when I saw a shell land right in front of a carrier. The vehicle rolled down a steep bank like a shot rabbit. I ran towards it but others closer got there before me. As I turned back for the farm a shell landed twenty yards behind me. I threw myself flat, surviving two more near-misses, then ran for the farm, wondering if I was going to be killed whilst L.O.B. Once in the farm I'll be O.K., I thought. I reached it at the same time as the enemy gunners. During the next ten minutes the farm was hit repeatedly. The Germans must have used the house as an

* Left out of Battle.

H.Q. then 'mapped it'. The presence of Major Freeman helped us stomach the shelling. Only a month previously he had been Lieutenant-Colonel Freeman, C.O. of a tank regiment. He had asked for a transfer because he wanted to find out what life in the infantry was like. The transfer had been arranged, with the inevitable loss of rank. Anyone ready to step down from Lieutenant-Colonel in order to join the infantry had us agog. During the stonk he shepherded us about with the air of someone who had the answer to it. It was going to take a lot to shake him.

At most I had imagined myself on a night-guard round the farm. Major Freeman soon spoiled that one. I and another L.O.B. were to act as guards for a mule-train carrying supplies to the Company. The muleteers would be Italian. We were to keep an eye out for pilfering, as well as Germans.

We set out at dusk. I watched the mules closely. Linked in pairs, their muleteers at their heads, they gave nothing away. Impassive as oxen, I decided. We were making our way along a flat piece of track, a bank to our left, a ravine on our right, when we got shelled. I was right in amongst the mules, and glad of it. Apart from protecting me from shrapnel they treated the shelling with the same indifference they showed to everything else. Until the one immediately in front of me was hit in the buttock. It charged towards the bank, taking its companion – on my right – with it. I jumped clear – on to the edge of the ravine. A 'haybox' of tea hurtled past me. I listened to it crashing amongst the rocks.

The muleteer soon had the team under control. He talked to them like a lover. But I had had enough, and spent the rest of the march well clear of them.

It was one o'clock before we reached the Company. They had taken over positions from the Guards about half a mile from the summit. They had had no contact with the enemy, and had not been shelled. The Platoon were amused to hear that we had.

The Company bumped soon after dawn. A patrol from Six Platoon was ambushed in dense undergrowth and their officer killed. The C.S.M. went out on a one-man retaliatory raid, and bombed an enemy trench. Later another patrol knocked out a Spandau post and took four prisoners. I heard all about it when I went up with the mule-train.

The following day Saddler and Wilson went out sniping. The enemy put a small mortar-bomb between Wilson's calves. He escaped with a flesh wound, and was sent out of battle.

After three nights with the mules Major Freeman told me I could take a rest. Someone woke me in the middle of the night. Guard, I thought sleepily, they think I'm on guard.

'I'm not on stag,' I murmured.

'You're going up the hill,' said the rifleman.

'I'm what! Going up the hill! I'm L.O.B.!'

'I know that. Three blokes have buggered off. The Company's going into an attack at eight o'clock, and Major Freeman's taking you and the other L.O.B. up as replacements.'

'Christ! What's the time?'

'Half two. You're moving off at three.'

As I dressed I asked who had deserted.

'I don't know their names but they're all from your Platoon.'

204

'Groves for one,' I thought. 'Meredith, probably, but who else?'

I had to unpack half the fifteen-hundredweight before I found my Tommy. This put me in the worst of tempers. As I walked back across the vehicle park a sentry challenged me. I had passed him on my way to the truck.

'For Christ's sake!' I snarled, 'can't you see it's me?'

'You give the password or else I'll fire,' said the sentry nervously.

That did it.

'You've got a rifle and I've got a Tommy!' I told him. 'We'll see who wins!'

Pointing the gun at his stomach I walked towards him. The sentry hastily grounded arms.

Major Freeman was waiting for me at the front door.

'I'm very sorry about this,' he said. 'The blighters followed the mule-train down. I wish I could deal with them myself.'

'Who are they?'

'White, Groves, and Sullivan.'

White was one of the 'base-wallah' brigade. Sullivan's desertion surprised me.

'We're due there at seven-fifteen,' said Major Freeman. 'We'll have to step on it.'

We did. By the time we neared the Company, I and the L.O.B. were panting like dogs. Major Freeman was walking as easily as ever. When the Platoon caught sight of me they cheered.

'The Teds 'ave 'ad it now!' shouted Page.

'You're just in time,' said Saddler. 'We put off the attack till you arrived.'

Jeffreys looked upset.

'I told them we could do without you,' he said. 'They wouldn't listen.'

I told him not to worry.

'I don't think they'll put up much of a fight,' said Jeffreys. 'Anyway we've got a Divisional stonk for once – every gun and mortar they've got.'

As he guided me to the section's positions I asked him why the three men had deserted.

'I took them out to a listening post in front of the Company. We got sniped and they bolted.'

I didn't need telling that the section's trenches had been dug by Guardsmen. They were five feet deep and beautifully finished. The smell of frying bacon interested me even more.

'Bacon!'

'And beans,' said Jeffreys. 'Owen is cook.'

Owen's cheerful face peered out of a trench.

'Are you hungry?' he asked.

'I'd say! I as good as ran up the bloody hill.'

As I took out my mess-tins some shells landed farther up the hill. I dropped into a trench.

'Anyone up there?' I asked Jeffreys.

'Six Platoon.'

There were no more shells. Owen was dishing up when Meadows came through the bushes holding two mess-tins.

'You've had a third of that,' he said. 'One of those shells landed in Six Platoon's breakfast.'

'Anyone hurt?'

'No. A couple of blokes got buried in a slit'un but they're O.K.'

After breakfast the attack was called off. The

enemy had pulled out, or so it was thought. The Platoon less me – Jeffreys saw to that – went out on a fighting patrol and confirmed that they had. The Turcomen had abandoned a dump of tinned food that would have done credit to Fortnum and Mason's reserve stocks. There was butter from Denmark, cheese from Holland, pilchards from Norway, chocolate and biscuits from France, meat, sugar, tea, and dehydrated cabbage – this proved to be delicious, unlike our own dehydrated potatoes – from Germany. The Platoon brought down as much as they could carry, and Major Dunkerley arranged for Major Freeman to load some of the rest on to the mules. So much for blackberries.

We met the mule-train on our way down. Major Freeman was leading it. We cheered him. Quick calculations showed that by the time he finished the round trip he would have covered eighty-odd miles in less than twenty hours.

'No wonder 'e wanted to join the infantry,' said Humphreys.

Wilson met us at the farm.

'Look at me war-wound!' he shouted, pulling up his trouserleg. 'Look at me war-wound!'

On his leg was a piece of Elastoplast the size of a half-crown.

'That makes three!' said Saddler, pointing accusingly at a fresh wound-stripe on Wilson's jacket. 'How about giving us one?'

'No one's going to have my wound-stripe,' piped Wilson in falsetto, and covered it up like a hen protecting her chicks.

He quickly switched back to covering us. He had

made sure we had got the most comfortable spot in the farm, and he made it seem like the Ritz. I fell asleep with him grinning at me.

The next day the Company moved to another farm. The C.O. had given the Platoon's deserters court-martials. We had to guard them in the meantime. They weren't allowed to smoke but they did just the same. Saddler was the only N.C.O. not to turn a blind eye to this. When he caught Sullivan having a pull he snatched the cigarette out of his mouth.

'Deserters don't smoke!' he said.

Sullivan told me that Jeffreys' fussing had got on his nerves.

'If he hadn't kept shooshing I'd have stuck,' he said.

The 'grapevine' reported that there were thirty thousand men in Italy 'on the trot'. I could well believe it. A rifleman on leave had gone back to Regello. When he'd offered an Italian a cigarette the man said: 'Thanks, mate. I'll 'ave the packet.' He was a deserter from 'C' Company. I wondered what the numbers would be when the weather broke. Jeffreys told me that the nights on Peschiena had been bitterly cold. Major Dunkerley had put in an urgent request for greatcoats. He got the same answer as before.

Two days later the Company moved on to another farm, shedding the deserters *en route*, and had a week's rest. I taught myself the German for 'Surrender or you'll be killed!' and one or two phrases that might come in handy if I were taken prisoner myself.

During the rest Meadows and Saddler had gone down with yellow jaundice, along with seven or eight others in the Company. We were told it was infectious. I wondered if lack of fresh fruit and vegetables had something to do with it. We had had nothing but tinned food for a month.

When we left the farm the farmer ran after us. The C.S.M. had pinched his wireless. Major Dunkerley made 'Bombhead' return it. The farmer had been very friendly, and quite apart from that the C.S.M. had broken the Company's code of looting – take from the rich, leave the peasants who billeted us alone.

On our way to yet another farm it began raining. The temperature dropped sharply. As we approached our billet we saw a company from the 5th under canvas, and blessed our luck at having a Commander who made sure we were always under a roof.

The new farm turned out to be very snug. Jeffreys and I passed the evening eating baked potatoes with the farmer's daughters. They told us that the Germans had moved out the previous week. I asked them what they were like. Nice, they said. But tired of war.

I thought of the Germans sitting where we were sitting, and saying the same sort of things. The war was bad enough for us. What must it be like for them? Always retreating, and knowing, most of them, that they had no hope of winning?

A storm sprang up in the night. It was still blowing next morning. It was still raining too. After breakfast Jeffreys and I stood watching it stream down the windows. The year's fall set off a wild train of sadness. I thought of the dead, unburied in the rain, of ourselves, waiting our turn, and of all the hapless futility of war.

'It makes you think, doesn't it?' said Jeffreys.

I looked round at him. Jeffreys stared straight ahead. His face was so sad I had to look away.

'You know,' he said slowly, 'I've had four years in a duty platoon. That's a long time. They've never given me a rest. There are lots of younger blokes at Tac H.Q. A spell there would be just right. The trouble is that once you prove yourself reliable they shit on you. They use you. They use you till you – '

He broke off with a shrug.

'Oh, well,' he said, smiling. 'Who knows? Perhaps I'll get one just the same.'

His words coming on top of my sadness brought me to the point of tears. There was nothing I could say. Perhaps I had drawn off some of his sadness. It felt like it. When he walked away I sat down on my blankets and wrote a sonnet called 'The Dead'. It came straight out, and the sadness passed into the words.

12
ORLANDO

It was the worst autumn in Italy for twenty years. Rain fell almost continuously, and in the mountains it turned to sleet. The men holding them were still in summer kit. One night a rifleman in the 1st Battalion died of exposure. Twelve others were carried down the mountain. The next day 'D' Company got its winter kit. We heard of its arrival at the same time as the death of the rifleman. Wilson called the Platoon together. He was white with anger.

'Last night one of the 1st died from exposure,' he said quietly, his voice only slightly off-key. 'Twelve others are in dock. Our winter kit arrives today.'

He looked each of us in the face. You've heard the news, his own said. Now for the comment.

'Some poor sod has to die before they pull their finger out!' he shouted.

We would remember the rifleman.

The Company was still in reserve, building a Jeep-truck in the mountains and carrying out O.P. patrols. The Platoon had taken over a small farm from the 5th. They had left us their trade-mark. Instead of digging a latrine they had squatted down in the yard. We had run into the Platoon responsible on our way to the farm. A more miserable-looking bunch would

211

be hard to find. This in spite of their having their own vehicles. I wondered if the luxury had gone bad on them.

A day or so later something seemed to have gone bad on me. The tank push the I.O. had told us about had been held up by rain – in places whole stretches of the road (there was only one) had been washed away – and this had enabled the enemy to sit tight in the mountains. Wilson warned the Platoon that the Company would lead a Battalion attack on a Monte Orlando. The news made me feel horribly depressed. It must be the weather, I thought. It'll pass in the night.

In the morning the depression was still with me. The arrival of two Christmas puddings failed to shift it. If Christmas puddings don't help, I thought, what will? Was I cracking up? It was a terrifying thought. Jeffreys and Owen did their best to wipe it out. There were still forty-eight hours to go before the attack, they argued. I would feel better by then. We now had a daily rum issue. I decided to save mine for the attack.

Meredith went about telling everyone he was going to be killed. I had much the same idea about myself, but some last-minute information gave me a lift. The enemy, Divisional Intelligence told us, consisted of 'Six men and a Spandau'. The Arezzo men yelled at this.

'Bet it's the same six!' shouted Humphreys.

Orlando lay conveniently close to the road. We could move to within half a mile of it by truck. Unluckily for us the Germans shelled the road just when we needed it. The shelling was too heavy to

212

risk a run through. By the time it stopped we were half an hour behind schedule. We went up Orlando like cross-country runners. Spiked shoes would have helped. The path was firm but very slippery. We shot about on it like novices on a skating-rink. But we kept the pace. This was partly due to Major Dunkerley, who kept dropping back to encourage us, but if we had been dumb we would never have managed it. We swore our way up Orlando. The cuss-words rose and fell with invocatory power. From the distance it must have sounded rather beautiful, like monks chanting plainsong.

Major Freeman, who had come a longer but easier way round, met us near the summit. He had brought a mule-load of tea and stew with him. It was only then that I discovered we weren't on Orlando at all. We were on a mountain overlooking it. Major Dunkerley had decided to approach Orlando from above. It seemed an excellent idea.

The forced march had cured my depression but I decided to take the rum just the same. After one swig I vomited all the stew. Humphreys drank the rest of the rum, and marvelled at the ways of providence.

We began the descent round the next corner. The rain had stopped, and we could pick out the summit of Orlando. It was absolutely flat, as if at some time its peak had fallen off. I had a hunch that the enemy had pulled out. They had. Major Dunkerley sent out a patrol to see if the Six Men had withdrawn to a farm on an adjoining mountain. We were not to dig in until ordered to. I curled up round a bush and went to sleep.

I woke up to a 'pop!' The summit lit up like Pic-

213

cadilly Circus. A Spandau opened up. Then more flares. And more Spandaus – a lot more. One of them traversed the Platoon's bushes. We got up and ran.

'Don't panic, Four Platoon!' yelled Wilson. 'They're firing over your heads!'

We subsided into some bushes just below the summit. As I went down I saw a giant rifleman silhouetted by a flare. He was wearing a steel helmet several sizes too small for him. It looked like a child's po.

The enemy began mortaring the summit. The Company began digging in. Major Dunkerley quickly told us to stop – the enemy might hear us. The mortaring seemed loud enough to cover any noise we might make, but if the enemy had suddenly stopped firing they could have picked us up. They obviously thought we were on the summit – they were probing every yard of it – and as long as they kept their bombs there we were safe. I was six feet below the summit, looking straight at it, when a bomb landed right on the edge, at the exact point I was watching. Before the shock hit me, in the split-second between the blast and my reaction to it, I saw two different shades of red – the dark-red of disintegrating metal, the funnel of flame opening round it. Then I went to bits myself. The reds of the explosion were clamped on my retina. For several minutes I could see nothing else. This plus the blast plus the fact that we couldn't dig in reduced me to jelly. Desert. Desert. Desert. The next time, I promised myself. The next time I will. Before the attack. A court-martial's better than this. I steadied myself by scratching the ground with my entrenching tool.

214

Our own twenty-fives' opened up. The mortaring and Spandauing grew heavier. The enemy must have thought we were attacking. A few yards below me Major Dunkerley was operating a field-telephone. As I watched he stood upright and began speaking.

'Hullo, Charles,' he drawled. 'I'm afraid we've run into a spot of bother.'

A spot of bother, I thought. Christ!

The Company Commander put the C.O. in the picture. His picture. He ignored the shrapnel. He cut the stuff dead. How the hell does he do it, I thought. Seconds after he had finished speaking one of the patrol who had bumped the enemy reported to him.

'I tripped a wire outside the house, sir,' said the rifleman. 'That set the first flare off. A Spandau opened up from close range. They must have been asleep. I threw two grenades and they stopped firing. I pulled out then. I don't know what happened to the rest of the patrol.'

All this in an easy, matter-of-fact tone of voice.

'Never mind,' said Major Dunkerley. 'You've done very well.'

He certainly had. Watching him and the Company Commander had done me a power of good. I had forgotten all about the near-miss.

Major Dunkerley whirled the handle of the field-telephone. The other end didn't answer. The C.S.M. bent over the box.

'It's duff, sir!' he said. 'Shrapnel!'

A signaller came up to try and mend it. He was still working on it when two more of the patrol reported. One of them was wounded.

'Shall I take him to the R.A.P., sir?' said his mate.

'No, I'll look after him!' said the C.S.M. before Major Dunkerley could answer. 'You go back to your Platoon!'

'Bombhead' was off like a shot. I watched him go. 'You won't be back, chum,' I thought. 'Not until the show's over.'

The enemy mortared the summit for three hours. Not one bomb fell on our side of it. For once the mortarmen's uncanny accuracy proved a blessing. When they stopped firing we listened anxiously. Would they put in an attack? Or send a patrol? They did neither. Digging in was now out of the question. We waited for Major Dunkerley to tell us to pull out. He took his time about it. At first light we still hadn't moved.

'If we stay here much longer they'll see the lot of us!' I whispered to Jeffreys.

'I suppose the C.O.'s told him to stay put.'

'Yes, that's the sort of thing he would say!'

For want of anything better to do I watched the day break. The mountains to the east stood out against the sky, those in between were bewilderingly similar. How the generals knew where they were I couldn't imagine.

As the black of the enemy-held mountain turned to grey the Company began to murmur. Major Dunkerley rang the C.O. and got permission to withdraw.

'He's left it too damn late,' I thought.

The grey had turned to green. It was dawn.

As I got to my feet I felt so sick I had to sit down again.

'I'll catch you up,' I told Jeffreys.

Last man out, I thought. There must be something wrong with me.

When I got up I could hardly believe my eyes. Major Dunkerley was leading the Company up the same knife-edged path we had used during the night. The men on it stuck out like ninepins. I looked round at the enemy's hill. Its green was dead sharp. Then I looked at the path leading to the R.A.P. The Company would have been safely out of sight on that. Why in God's name hadn't he taken it?

The effort I had to make to walk astonished me. I had to bend double to keep going. All the time I was listening for the enemy mortars. I heard them fire. The bombs landed well up the mountain. Crouching behind a rock I watched the next batch. The first bomb burst to the left of the Company, the second to its right. The third landed in the middle of them. I looked away, sick at heart.

When I looked up again the Company had disappeared. I climbed slowly after them. It seemed unlikely that the enemy would try and hit one man. Rounding a bend I came across half a dozen wounded. They had been hit in the legs. The chief medical orderly was with them.

'You O.K.?' he said. 'Tell Major Dunkerley to send some stretcher-bearers, will you? Mine ran for it.'

I began picking my way through the wounded. I needed all my strength to get one foot clear of the ground. The last man got trodden on. He yelled with pain. I had stepped on his wound. Oh, God, I thought.

'Sorry, chum,' I said. 'I couldn't help it.'

He glared at me as if he didn't believe it. Small wonder.

Stepping over the men had left me very weak. I had to bend till my head was level with my knees before I could go on. I saw nothing except the ground below my face. Nothing else until Meredith's face looked into mine. His eyes were glazed in terror. His mouth was open. He was screaming. Soundlessly. I waited for the sound. I could help then. It took a second or so to realize it would never come. Meredith was dead. Buried to the waist. The base-plug of the bomb lay beside him. As I straightened up I saw his arms. They stuck up like a drowning man's. Avoiding them I shuffled on up the path.

The problems of keeping going soon blocked out Meredith. But then it began raining. It was the last straw. I burst into tears. A moment later I spotted two men coming down the path. We waved to one another. The tears were forgotten. As the men drew nearer I recognized one of them as an officer from 'C' Company.

'You look rough,' he said.

'I'm all right. Where on earth are you going?'

'To Orlando. To see if it's occupied.'

'Christ, we've only just left the bloody place!'

'I know. But the C.O. wants a fresh report.'

The C.O. wants shooting, I thought.

'You want to get off the path for a start,' I told the officer. 'They've got it taped.'

'And watch out when you get to the summit,' I added, as they stepped into the bushes.

'Oh, we'll be all right,' said the officer, with a fare-well grin.

As he spoke I felt certain he would be killed. His sergeant would be the one to be all right. Imminence

218

of death. I had never felt it about anyone before.

We exchanged a final wave. As they disappeared I walked on up the path. The 'C' Company Officer was a lovely man, as O'Connor would have said, one of the best. I cursed the C.O.

'It's a pity the bastard didn't go himself!' I shouted at the mountain.

In the same way as we had sworn our way up it the previous night so now I swore my way up its other side. I felt much better for it.

Below the summit I passed through 'C' Company's outposts. 'D' Company were a few hundred yards farther on, in a clearing. I emerged from some bushes right in front of the Platoon. Their eyes opened wide. None of them moved. They just stared.

'I can't look *that* ill,' I thought.

Then Jeffreys sprang forward.

'We thought you were dead,' he said. 'You were reported killed.'

'It was Meredith,' I said automatically.

Together we joined the Platoon, who were getting used to the idea that I was still alive. I had an eerie feeling myself.

'Anyone hurt?' I asked Jeffreys.

'Two of the new blokes. Not badly. They walked down to the A.D.S. Slim's missing.'

'He's not!'

'Someone slung the 2-inch mortar and he went back to find it.'

'He'll be back.'

I was quite certain he would be.

When I reported to Major Dunkerley he told me that stretcher-bearers were already on their way to the wounded.

'I'm glad to see you're still around,' he added.

On my way back to the Platoon I was overcome by a wave of nausea. With it came a depression that sliced at the very roots of my morale. I lay down on the ground without bothering to button my gas-cape. Let the rain do its worst. I was past caring. Major Dunkerley glanced at me curiously. I stared back. I didn't care what he thought. I didn't care if I lived or died.

When the wounded were brought in Humphreys asked me to help carry one of them down the mountain. After a few yards I nearly fainted.

'You'll have to find someone else,' I told him.

He gave me a dirty look. You can think what you bloody well like, I thought, and lay down again. I stayed there until Major Freeman arrived with a hot meal. 'C' Company's patrol was two hours overdue. Wilson had not returned either. This didn't worry me at all. I wondered why I was so certain he was all right.

Stew and tea did me good. I buttoned my cape and went to sleep. A burst of cheering woke me. Wilson stood on the edge of the clearing, the mortar slung over his shoulder, acknowledging the cheers with a wave and a grin. The man seemed like a god. He spanned our little world as no one else could. As long as he was with us – and I had no doubt he always would be – it didn't seem to matter so much what happened to the rest of us. He would see to it that we weren't forgotten. We would live through him.

During the afternoon the C.O. paid us a visit. He looked sick with worry. The hate I felt for him dried up.

Soon after dark 'C' Company's sergeant reported back. The officer had been shot dead as soon as they had reached Orlando. A patrol led by the Company Commander, Major Henderson, went out to recover the body. They passed through our lines. That the dead officer had been loved we knew. The patrol's faces showed the extent of the love. When they returned with the body 'D' Company began the descent of the mountain. We were heading for a farm at its foot. The track we took had turned into a mudbath. The darkness of the night conspired with the mud. Together they submerged us. We sploshed along wearily, one leg in, one leg out, like machines in need of new parts. A glimmer of light seemed like the Promised Land. Let it be ours, I prayed. It was. On the threshold of the farm I tripped and fell face-first in the mud. Jeffreys had to help me up.

The C.S.M. was in command of the farm. You found yourself the right job, didn't you, I thought.

'You're for guard, Bowlby!' he said.

'You'll have to find someone else. I'm not up to it,' I told him.

We looked at one another. Go on, I thought, just try and use your rank. 'Bombhead' thought better of it. Stripping myself naked I wrapped myself in a blanket. I felt very ill. Booth began talking about Meredith, how he'd known he was going to be killed. I reminded him that Meredith had said the same thing before Peschiena. Booth was still talking about him when I fell asleep.

The next morning the Company were preparing to climb back up the mountain when 'Bombhead' spotted a rifleman who, along with several others, had deserted

221

before the battle. The rifleman, an undersized lad who had deserted with Coke before Arezzo, had just slipped back amongst his Platoon – they were standing on a part of a track that had a drop of four feet – when the C.S.M. saw him.

'You bloody deserter!' he shouted, and charged towards him.

The deserter cringed. 'Bombhead' punched him in the stomach, then knocked him right off the path. The Company watched in silence. The news of 'Bombhead's' R.A.P. act had got around. I had seen to that. It made the tough stuff doubly nauseating.

As two of his mates helped the deserter to his feet the C.S.M. walked back to the farm. Our disgust hit him half-way. He glared back at us, then dropped his eyes and hurried indoors.

'He's a brave bugger, isn't he?' said Wilson.

We went up the mountain by a less muddy track and dug-in. First thing I had felt much better. The digging brought on more nausea. Jeffreys found me looking very sorry for myself.

'We're going to fetch Meredith,' he said. 'Do you feel up to giving us a hand?'

The thought of handling a corpse made me feel sicker than ever.

'Quite honestly I don't, Judge,' I told him.

'Afraid of a dead man, you are!' shouted Morgan.

'That's enough, Morgan!' said Jeffreys. 'It's quite O.K., Alec. I'll find someone else.'

But I was already getting out of my trench.

'I'll come, Judge, don't worry!' I told him.

I could have killed Morgan.

Owen completed the party. When they reached

the spot we found that someone had dug up the body and covered it with a gas-cape. It had already begun to decay. Owen took off his camouflage smock to use as a stretcher. He and Jeffreys rolled the body on to it. As all four of us bent down to lift the smock Morgan backed away.

'I cannot touch it, man!' he said.

'Yes, you bloody well can!' I said. 'Go on, get hold of that corner!'

Morgan got hold of it.

All this time we were under observation by the enemy. They honoured our role, just as they had at Arezzo.

We buried Meredith in the Company's clearing. Major Dunkerley read the burial service, and some-one made a cross out of a provisions' box. No one had liked Meredith but he had been one of us. We mourned him for that, and for his grave in the mountains. His body might never be found. No one would visit this grave. As he had been lonely in life so he would be lonely in death. The rain rubbed it in. If I'm killed let it be near a town, I prayed, so that I'll be remembered.

An hour before dusk the Company withdrew to another farm. A stream ran past it. Major Freeman had a dip in it.

In the morning, after another dip, he took Jeffreys' section up the mountain. We were to establish an O.P. there. The rest of the Company stayed below.

Whilst we watched the enemy shell the valley road Major Freeman told us that Divisional Intelligence now admitted that Orlando was held by a battalion. 'A' Company had taken a mountain on its flank, and had beaten off several counter-attacks. The tanks were going to try and outflank Orlando by road. We saw them try, a whole line of them. The shelling forced them to take shelter under the lee of a hill overhanging one side of the road. They stayed there all day. I had never seen anything quite so static as that long line of tanks.

Just before we withdrew I discovered another dead rifleman lying in some bushes. He didn't belong to the Company. Yet 'C' Company had reported no one missing. He had no Pay-Book and no identity discs. Major Freeman made arrangements to get him buried.

We got back to the farm in time for dinner. I felt too sick to eat and went to bed, on a marvellous feather-bed I shared with Booth and Owen. In the morning Owen brought me breakfast in bed. Wilson looked in as well.

'You're to report sick,' he said. 'That's an order.'

Now the Company were out of battle I felt easier about leaving it. My farewells were brief and light-hearted.

'See you in a couple of days!' I shouted.

On my way to the A.D.S. I stopped at Tac H.Q. for a cup of tea. A sergeant from the Intelligence Corps was already having one. I eyed him with interest.

'You on a special job?' I asked.

'Yes. I'm going to see if Orlando's still occupied.'

Well, well, I thought.

'You'd better watch it,' I said.

'Oh, I'll be all right.'

The same words. This time I had no intimations. I just wished him luck.

As I walked into the near R.A.P. – it was in a house on the roadside – the enemy shelled it. I flattened myself against the wall. The orderlies dived under a table. This amused me. But they had reason to be afraid.

'We've 'ad a time!' one of them told me. 'They're shelling every bleeding thing. They can't see the Red Cross. And they just hit the Lancer's H.Q. round the corner. It was shell-proof, they reckoned. Something about the angle of the 'ill and the angle of the guns. Well the Teds put a shell right bang in the C.O.'s office. It went through into the living quarters. Eight blokes killed and seventeen wounded.'

An M.O. examined my eyes and urine.

'You've got jaundice,' he said.

Five minutes later I was in an ambulance, beside the driver.

'They're knocking shit out of the road,' he said. 'We're going through flat out.'

We belted down the road, shells landing fore and aft. I was too busy admiring the skill of the driver to be afraid. To touch 65 m.p.h. on a road jam-packed with craters is quite something.

The A.D.S. was alongside the Company's vehicle park. I went to collect some extra kit and ran into O'Connor. When he heard I had jaundice he shouted for joy.

'You're laughing, Alec!' he said. 'You're laughing! You'll be out of the shit for five or six weeks!'

This staggered me. I had no idea it was such a long business.

When I reported to the A.D.S. an orderly led me into a combined waiting and operating-room. Some of the most seriously wounded Lancers were being operated on by two tired-looking M.O.s.

'They've been at it since seven o'clock this morning,' whispered the orderly.

It was now three p.m.

After a short wait I boarded a second ambulance. We were bound for the 6th (South African) General Hospital in Florence.

13
FLOWERS OF THE FOREST

The 6th S.A. had a marvellous atmosphere – warm, friendly, and *sans* bullshit. The two M.O.s who made the rounds of my ward might have been treating private patients.

'You're in the infantry, aren't you?' said the one who examined me (the other sat on the bed, grinning). 'Well, you're going back for a good rest. You've deserved it.'

He clapped me on the shoulder, and moved on.

The next day I went to a small British hospital south of Florence. It was a come-down after the 6th S.A. – anything would have been – but things were pleasantly informal. Unluckily for them and for me the Guards got cut up in a big attack and my bed was needed. Another ambulance took me to a hospital ship at Ancona. We were bound for Bari. For a British base hospital. I didn't like the sound of that.

My first morning in the hospital the Sergeant in charge of my ward suddenly shouted 'Lie to attention!'

I looked up in astonishment. A Sister walking down the ward caught my eye.

'Come along there!' she said. 'Arms by your side! Legs together! The M.O.'ll be here any minute!'

The great man examined me as if I was a rather

uninteresting piece of machinery, said a few words to the Sister, and moved on to the next bed.

A Red Cross Sister, the hospital librarian, came round one day when I was smoking my pipe.

'You got that at Bacon's, in Cambridge!' she exclaimed.

I had, too. She sat down on the bed, and told me about her brother, who had a similar pipe, and we talked about Cambridge, the war, and many other things. The next time she came round the ward she cut me dead. Presumably she had been seen fraternizing with an 'other rank', and had been warned that this was just not done. A nymphomaniac night-nurse who had a habit of stripping the Sergeant's bed clothes off him got away with it. The Sergeant had long conversations with the Corporal in the next bed about reporting her. He never did.

The hospital Matron, a stubby old battle-axe who paved the way for the C.O.'s inspections, invariably found something wrong with my kit display. Our hospital blues were supposed to jell with a white shirt and a red tie, and form a set 'flag'. Mine never did. One morning the Matron pulled the whole thing to bits.

'What a mess!' she said.

I prayed silently. Behind the flag I had hidden my boots. They were still caked with Orlando mud. An inch thick. I had left them that way deliberately. They provided me with a link with 'D' Company, and a snook at the hospital.

'There!' said the Matron. 'This is how they should look.'

Then she saw the boots. Her eyes bulged.

Here it comes, I thought.

'You *are* a naughty boy!' said the Matron, more awed than angry. 'Hide them quickly before the C.O. comes!'

I just managed it in time. Not that it mattered. The old boy could hardly see us, let alone our kit. After the inspection the Matron came back with a tin of boot-polish. And for another look at the boots. They fascinated her. I don't think anyone else had pulled anything quite like it.

When I removed the mud, using the back of a brush and old razor-blades, I found the leather had turned green. No amount of blacking changed this. They remained green for the rest of their days.

At no time during my three weeks in hospital did I have the usual jaundice depression. I had got shot of most of it before and during Orlando, and what was left was transmuted by my satisfaction at being out of the fighting. I missed the Platoon badly, and I missed the setting of the Company, but this in no way diminished the relief of knowing that for many days to come I was certain of being alive.

Between reading, writing letters, thinking about the Company, and gossiping with my next-door neighbours, I looked back over the months. Chance had spared me what I dreaded most – hand-to-hand fighting and seeing men blown to bits. In only one department of war could I call myself fully experienced. I had learnt quite a bit about courage. I could tell at a glance what a man would be like in a tight spot. A Wilson or a Baker could get a widow's mite from most men. Those who had been unable to give it – Coke, and the rest – had been 'closed' men, shut off from the tribal spirit that kept the rest of us going. They had fallen because of this. My own immediate source of courage – fear of disgrace – would soon have dried up without it. When I considered how Baker and Wilson had fostered this spirit in the Platoon, and how Captain Kendall had done the same for the Company, it made me realize how infinitely greater their achievement had been than officers and N.C.O.s in units like Commandos and Paratroops, whose duds were quickly sent back to their former units, and whose standard of replacements – this was the key to the whole business – was always high (the Guards had picked replacements). A private in the next bed to me told me about an unfortunate county battalion made up of 'any old shit', as he put it, and brigaded with Indian troops. The whole Battalion had cut and run from a German tank attack. The Indians recaptured the ground. Once the Brigade was out of the Line the English Brigadier formed both Battalions into a square, the Indians on the outside, with their weapons, the county regiment inside, without weapons. He then told them what he thought of them. What must it have been like to be a good officer or N.C.O. in a Battalion like that?

I left hospital in the middle of November. I was very glad to do so. This, unless I'm much mistaken, was what I was intended to feel. The South African hospital authorities believed that a hospital should be a pleasant place. The British used the 'Make it rough so they won't malinger' approach. At least that's what I and every other rank I talked to thought.

The local convalescent camp was run on much the

same lines. In a way this helped. I had softened up alarmingly. The thought of going into action worried me far more than it had between battles (Orlando excepted). The 'few days in, few days out' policy of the top brass had left no time for softening. Along with the angst came a craving for a woman. Fear of V.D., and its consequences, prevented me from looking for one. (The powers-that-be categorized V.D. as a self-inflicted wound.)

After a week's convalescence I went to an Infantry Training Depot near Naples (out of bounds owing to the V.D. rate). 'Make it rough – or they'll get our jobs' was the staff's guiding principle. It worked very well. Each morning long queues of men petitioned their Company Commanders to send them back to their units. But this could only happen when the units asked for replacements.

One morning I saw a rifleman from 'D' Company. Had there been many casualties? I asked.

'No,' he said. 'It's been pretty cushy. But Corporal Jeffreys is dead. He stepped on a Teller, and it went off. He was on patrol.'

I walked away quickly, automatically heading for a wood outside the camp. There I sobbed my heart out. I felt as if part of myself had died.

By the evening the grief had bottled itself up. It stayed that way until one November evening fourteen years later, when I cried my way across half London.

After ten days at the I.T.D. I went north with a draft of riflemen, to another training depot near Arezzo. As soon as I arrived I saw Saddler sitting outside a bivouac.

'Dick!' I shouted.

'Hullo, Alec,' he said, without even a show of warmth.

This hurt. Then I realized that something had happened to Saddler. His eyes were all wrong. He grinned at me, an awful, twisted grin.

'You know Slim's dead?' he said.

The shock left me dumb.

'That cunt Booth,' said Saddler. 'Shot him in the back. They'd just come back from a patrol. Booth was cleaning the Bren. The Germans would never have got Slim. It had to be someone like Booth.'

A camp N.C.O. called me. I was too numbed to answer. He called me again, angrily.

'Better go, Alec,' said Saddler.

The camp was a bad one, even by training depot standards. It was under canvas, and under water – the rain saw to that. The camp N.C.O.s made us march to dinner, although this meant that we had to use a track where the water came up over our ankles. There was a dry short-cut but we weren't allowed to use it. The daily sick-list reached such a size that the M.O. warned the C.O. that unless the camp was shifted there would be an epidemic. Two days later we moved into an empty brick factory. In the interim I ran into a rifleman from the 1st Battalion. I hadn't seen him since Egypt.

'What was all that I heard about that blooming great pipe of yours?' he said. 'About some bloke picking it up in the middle of a stonk?'

The tale had got around.

Physically, the factory was a great improvement. Atmospherically things were much the same. The C.O. employed all available other ranks building a path to the officers' mess. Out on a tour of inspection he found four riflemen sitting down playing cards.

'What the devil do you think you're doing!' he exclaimed.

''aving a game of nap,' said one of the riflemen, without bothering to get up.

The next morning the rifleman was on a charge. 'There's something up!' he told us. 'I told the old geezer if 'e didn't send me back to the Battalion I'd desert. "That won't be necessary," he says. "You'll be going there quick enough." '

Camp N.C.O.s descended on us. All riflemen were at two hours' notice to move. The Q.M. would start issuing kit right away.

One rumour had it that the enemy had broken through the Brigade's front, another that we had broken through the enemy's. The air of suppressed panic made it clear which was the most probable. The rifle draft moved off after lunch. By then we were down to facts. One of our three Battalions had been badly cut up in an attack.

The Brigade was operating in the mountains to the north-east of Florence. Disaster or not we spent the night at a transit-camp in the foothills beyond the city. There we saw an open-air showing of the film 'Fanny by Gaslight'. One of the tents caught fire in the middle, so we had a live show as well.

In the morning we drove over the great Borgo San Lorenzo pass, arriving at Brigade H.Q. in time for lunch. The cooks were in a panic.

'The 3rd's wiped out!' one of them said. 'They're all killed and wounded! The 5th's 'ad a bashing – there's only the 1st between us and the Teds!'

233

His hands were shaking so much he put half my stew on the grass.

'Windy bastards!' said Saddler. 'Things can't be that bad.'

We reached Battalion H.Q.'s village in the late afternoon. The first person I saw was the Adjutant, with whom I had been at school. He was staring out of the window at nothing. His face told a much more convincing tale than the cook's.

O'Connor met the truck. We walked off by ourselves. What he had to tell me was, inevitably, only half the story. My own account of the battle is based on (1) Information I picked up immediately after it. (2) Eye-witness accounts from men taken prisoner during the battle. (3) The official Regimental history.

On the night of December 12th/13th 'D' and 'C' Companies, supported by 'B' Company had attacked a small town called Tossignano.* Part of the support barrage had fallen on 'C' Company, and killed or wounded a whole Platoon. The remaining Platoons led by Major Freeman, commanding the Company, had fought their way into the town, whose natural defences – Tossignano lies on top of a great bluff of rock – proved as awkward as the defenders. 'D' and 'B' Companies followed on. By midday – the attack had gone in at 3 a.m. – most of the town had been taken. As Major Freeman was leading a final thrust he and his two remaining Platoon Commanders

* This was an insignificant little place but it happened to be one of two key-points of the Gothic Line which were attacked within twenty-four hours of one another, the chances being that if both attacks were successful the Gothic would be wide open. The second attack also failed.

234

were severely wounded by mortar-bombs. This disaster forced the Company on to the defensive. In spite of his wounds – one of his legs was amputated after the battle – Major Freeman continued to direct operations with supreme confidence. In the late afternoon he reported that the Company was holding its own, and would continue to do so. Major Dunkerley had also been badly shot up. By the end of the day's fighting there was only one unwounded officer left in the Battalion. Water had run out, and ammunition was low.

During the night parties from Battalion rear H.Q. ('A' Company were committed elsewhere) tried to bring up ammunition. They found that the enemy had cut the supply line. One officer, loaded with ammunition, ran the gauntlet. He arrived with one arm partly shot away, but fought alongside the Platoon he supplied all the next day.

The situation was critical. And the enemy (the Battalion involved, the 1st Battalion 755th, had been described by British Army Intelligence as belonging to the best enemy infantry division in Italy) exploited the 3rd's one glaring weakness – lack of inter-platoon wireless communication – with great skill. The 3rd's Company wireless sets, the '69s', could communicate with rear H.Q. only. The Platoon wireless sets were not capable of transmitting through the walls of the houses, so none of the Platoons could communicate with one another. This prevented any sort of co-ordinated defence, and enabled the enemy to infiltrate into the houses between the Platoons. One by one the defenders were sealed off. The enemy then brought up pioneers to burn them out.

On the night of December 14th/15th the Brigadier laid on an attack by the 5th. The leading Company took a short cut and got lost. The second one did not get used until twenty-four hours later – twenty-four hours too late. When the 'lost' Company arrived they needed a rest. The attack went in much later than planned. One Platoon fought their way into the town, and linked up with the 3rd.

Communications between Major Freeman and Battalion rear H.Q. ceased in the early hours of December 15th. At 2 p.m. Major Dunkerley also went off the air. When the 5th's second Company attacked they achieved some success but it was clear from the strength of the enemy's resistance, and from the absence of any fire-fight except between them and the 5th, that the 3rd had been overcome.

The Brigade's casualties totalled thirteen officers and two hundred and seven other ranks. Of these twenty-three were killed, sixty wounded and evacuated during the battle, and the rest, many of them wounded, taken prisoner. Major Freeman was awarded the D.S.O. Williams, the rifleman I had seen report to Major Dunkerley at Orlando, was recommended for the V.C. for rescuing wounded under fire. He received the D.C.M. The Divisional Commander described the attack as 'a magnificent failure'.

O'Connor's 'grapevine' had it that the C.S.M. had been found dead outside the village, shot in the back – we wondered if he'd been trying the same R.A.P. act as he'd done at Orlando – and that Zwolski, our friend of Perugia days, had been buried alive by the Germans, a ghastly fulfilment of O'Connor's crack about what the Germans would do if they ever caught him. After the war a sergeant who had fought in the same house as Zwolski told me that the Germans *had* buried him alive, but not in the way one imagined. Their pioneers had placed Teller mines on one of the walls of the house, and blown it down. Zwolski had been buried and killed by the falling debris. The same sergeant also cleared up the circumstances of the C.S.M.'s death. When the battle was nearing its end, and surrender inevitable, Bombhead had decided to make a run for it. 'Nothing's going to stop my home leave,' he'd said. And off he'd gone.

When O'Connor had finished telling me what he knew about the battle we sat staring into a river.

'There was a jinx on us all right,' said O'Connor.

'It was a shame about "Judge", wasn't it?' he continued softly. 'They ought to put up a memorial to men like "Judge".'

Why Judge? I thought. Why not Wilson? It took me years to realize why.

The C.O. had gone home on leave in November. It took me even longer to realize what the result of the battle, and his not being there, must have meant to him.

Of the men from the 3rd who had fought their way into the town, as opposed to those who had taken part in the attack – there had been a score or more who had got 'lost' on the way in – only two had fought their way out again. One of them was Corporal Bailey. He had been wounded in one arm but had insisted on seeing those of 'D' Company who had missed the battle, before he went to hospital. What he told us hasn't stuck. I remember something about wounded men trapped in a burning church, nothing else. Bailey himself is clear enough. He chronicled the end of things with an intensity that bit like a whip. Before he began he looked straight at me. Child that I was I hoped for some sort of encouragement. This time he had none to spare. There's a gulf now, I thought. Between those who were in the battle and those who weren't. The gulf could have been of my own making. It didn't seem like it at the time.

Soon after Bailey had left O'Connor brought me a letter. He had an odd look on his face.

The letter was one I had sent my cousin, a subaltern in the Warwicks, and the only person of my own background to whom I was close. On the back someone had written 'This officer has been killed in action'.

14
'THE OX SHALL BE BURIED'

The 3rd had lost nearly two-thirds of its fighting strength. No extra replacements were available. The Battalion had to re-organize on a two-company basis. In the meantime it was pulled out of the Line.

A new 'D' Company spent Christmas in a country-house near Florence. The Germans sent us a card – they shelled the 1st and 5th with propaganda leaflets headed 'The Rifle Regiment attack!' 'Hundreds of dead and wounded are lying before our lines!' wrote the copy-writer, understandably light-headed at the chance of describing a victory. On the back of the leaflet, under the headline 'These men will enjoy a safe Christmas in Germany – why not join your pals?' was a list of prisoners. All the missing members of Four Platoon, including Sergeant Meadows, who had 'deserted' from a convalescent camp to get back to the Battalion, were accounted for. Morgan had lost an eye, but none of the Platoon had been killed. Apart from Saddler, O'Connor, and myself the new Four Platoon included six other old hands – Booth and Page, who had both been in hospital at the time of the battle, two riflemen from H.Q. section who had taken part in the early stages of the attack and had then been 'cut off' – I began asking one of them about the battle but soon realized it was kinder to stop – and two of the base wallahs who had joined the Platoon before Orlando. This pair, two of the oldest soldiers in the business, had gone on leave just before the battle. If leave vacancies had not been so carefully controlled I would have said they had worked it.

There was enough beer and old faces for us to put a front on things. Major Robins, the new O.C., and the biggest card in the Battalion, sang 'Lili Marlene' in German, Major Henderson did a dance with his batman, and I, under pressure, sang 'Come Landlord fill the flowing bowl'. For some reason this had everybody in fits.

On January 1st the Company, less eleven deserters, mostly Tossignano survivors from 'C' Company, moved up the Line. After a hair-raising 'mad mile' – we missed our lot of shells by about ten seconds – we marched into the hills facing one side of Tossignano.

Four Platoon took over a farmhouse – from the 5th – half a mile from the town. Since the attack the R.A.F. had bombed it. The ruins stuck out like a broken tooth. The cliffs on which they rested were several hundred feet high. Seeing them made me realize what the Battalion had been up against.

The 5th hadn't bothered to fortify the farm. We set about doing this, watched by the farmer and his wife. He was eighty-four and she was seventy-nine. They had refused to leave the farm. When we stuffed a window up with sacks of grain the farmer blew his top. Luckily for us his wife saw the point – better damp grain than grenades through the window – and persuaded him to let us use the sacks. There was something touching about the old man's naïvety. If the Germans cared to they could have shelled the farm to bits. (They didn't do so because they knew our gunners would do the same to their farms. Both sides had settled down to a limited live-and-let-live.) The old man went about things as if they didn't exist. Each morning he took his ox out for water. This meant a trip of fifty yards in full view of the Germans. They let him be. They probably got a big kick out of seeing him as we did.

On the night of January 2nd–3rd we had two feet of snow. Under cover of a ground mist the Platoon snowballed furiously. Not much other fighting to be done in this, we thought.

We weren't far wrong. The snow took some getting used to. The first night-patrol the Platoon sent out got up to their necks in drifts. It took them eight hours to make a round trip of three miles. Their objective, another farm, was occupied only by its owners. (We were lucky. Ten days later the Guards lost four killed and ten wounded at the same farm.) I watched the patrol come in. When I challenged the leading man waved his arm.

'Good old Slim!' I thought.

At once I realized my mistake. The leading man was the new officer, but he had waved his arm just as Wilson had done at Orlando. I mention the incident because it shows how difficult it was to think of him as dead.

For a while the enemy contented himself with shooting up the farm with a Spandau. He began as soon as it was dark. Once I was on guard behind the front door when a bullet hit it. The 'clonk!' – it

sounded like a brick, as it had at Laterino – upset the
farmer's wife.

'*Paura!*' she moaned. '*Mi paura!*'

I told her that I was afraid, too. So was the German
who fired the shot. We were all afraid. After some
hesitation the old woman decided I might have
something, and went on cooking the dinner.

One night the enemy raided Five Platoon's farm,
just to the left of ours, and lost one man killed. The
next night they penetrated a mile behind Company
H.Q.'s farm, well to the rear of ours, and ambushed
our mule-train. Company H.Q. got the wind-up.
Major Robins ordered Four Platoon to provide them
with an extra guard. Saddler, Page, and I got the job.
We were furious. Company H.Q. had done no
patrols – 'specialists don't do patrols' we had been
told – and Saddler had seen three of them drunk on
our rum ration.

We were a couple of hundred yards from the farm
when Saddler spotted two men near some haystacks.

'Fox!' he bellowed.

The men slipped behind the stacks.

'They must be Teds!' said Saddler. 'If we're quick
we'll nab 'em!'

'Sod you,' I thought.

Saddler led us straight for them through virgin
snow – we made a noise like cows treading on glass,
an unpleasant surprise this – but when we reached
the stacks they'd gone.

'They must have hopped it,' said Saddler disap-
pointedly. 'We'll go round the farm, just in case.'

We ended up twenty yards from the front-door.
Nobody challenged us. We looked at the windows

curiously.

'I wonder?' said Saddler.

'You don't think the Teds have nabbed the lot!' I exclaimed.

'That's just what I was thinking!'

We grinned at one another.

'We'll soon find out,' said Saddler. 'Come on.'

We walked towards the house. Still nobody challenged. When we reached the front-door Saddler put an ear to it.

'There's someone inside!' he whispered. 'We're going in!'

He turned the handle soundlessly, then flung the door open. Major Robins was crouching behind a table, clutching a revolver. Beside him an equally pop-eyed C.S.M. For a moment both sides just stood and stared. Then the C.S.M. leapt forward.

'Come in quick!' he hissed. 'There's an enemy patrol outside!'

'No there ain't,' said Saddler.

'Don't argue!' said the C.S.M. 'Upstairs, Bowlby! There's a window overlooking the front-door – get on it!'

I found two signallers – specialists – by the window. They had grenades in each hand, but their arms were shaking so much they might have been castanets.

'There's a German patrol outside!' whispered one of them. 'We're surrounded!'

'No we're not,' I told them. 'We've been right round the place. There're no Germans for miles.'

'We seen 'em!' said the signaller. 'We seen 'em!'

I settled myself by the window. Petrified specialists warmed my heart. Then Saddler joined me. He was quivering with suppressed laughter.

'The silly sops!' he whispered. 'You know what happened? I got the password wrong. Should have been "Wolf" instead of "Fox". Those blokes we saw were Robbie and the C.S.M. When I called "Fox" they thought we were Teds, and scarpered back here.'

We rolled about on the floor, trying not to laugh out loud.

'I told them what must have happened' – continued Saddler. 'But they're going out to have another look. Just to make sure. I'd better get down there.'

As he left the front-door creaked open. Major Robins and the C.S.M. crept out trying to look all ways at once. They slunk along the front of the farm, and disappeared round the corner. Two minutes later they reappeared round the other corner. As nervous as ever. The C.S.M. was an old acquaintance. I decided to tickle him up. Instead of challenging at once I let them stumble on until they were right under the window.

'Wolf!' I shouted.

They jumped with shock.

'Why didn't you challenge before?' said the C.S.M. furiously.

'I wanted to make quite sure I didn't miss you, sir, if you were the enemy.'

'I see,' said the C.S.M., breathing hard.

He knew when he was beaten.

In the morning I had another sort of encounter.

One side of H.Q.'s farm overlooked a stretch of road held by the enemy. Two young O.P. officers were watching it with a more-than-routine interest.

'We're going to fix a D.R.!' one of them told me. 'He comes pissing along at five to nine each morning – we time our watches by him. We've fixed up a Divi. stonk, one round from each gun!'

I masked my feelings as best I could. O.P. officers could afford to treat war as a sport. We could not. It was a matter of distance, nothing more.

One of the officers lent me a pair of field-glasses, and pointed out the place of execution. The rider was on time. As one of the officers shouted down the telephone I watched him streak along the road. And prayed. The guns fired. Road and rider disappeared in smoke. When it cleared the rider was still moving. The next moment he was safely out of sight. I burst out laughing. The officers looked glum.

That night one of Four Platoon's riflemen shot a rabbit in mistake for a German. The night following Five Platoon warned us that they had seen a two-legged patrol heading our way. We stood-to at once. Watson and I were in the loft, behind a vent-hole just big enough to get one's head through. If the enemy came round our side of the house we could lob grenades at them. I say 'we' but it should really be 'I'. Stand-to or not Page slept.

A steady crunch-crunch-crunch made me jump. I pulled the pin of a grenade and kicked Page awake.

'They're right outside!' I whispered.

Page grunted sleepily. Crunch-crunch-crunch went the boots – but they hadn't got any closer. The Germans would hardly be marking time. Crunch-crunch-crunch. No louder. If it isn't Germans, I thought, it's not rabbits. I had two alternatives – to literally stick my neck out and try and see what it was or to lob the grenade. The lobbing was safe, but I didn't fancy rivalling the rabbit-shooting rifleman. Taking a deep breath I stuck my neck out. An enormous drop of rain hit it. I listened to other drops crunching into the snow – the vent-hole had magnified the sound – then pulled my head in.

'It was rain!' I told Page.

But he was sound asleep. When I went to put the pin back in the grenade I couldn't. I went on trying until the hand holding the safety-lever went numb. Should I throw the bomb? Or wake Page? Either way I'd be a laughing-stock. After resting my wrist against the ground I tried again. After a good half-hour I managed it. Then, and only then, did I realize that there had been no need to push the pin back. I could have unscrewed the base-plug and removed the fuse. This was too rich to keep to myself. I woke Page and told him what had happened. For the rest of our stay at the farm I was known as 'The Grenade King'.

Not content with their nightly Spandau spray the enemy began sniping us by day. This worried no one except the new Platoon officer, who thought something should be done about it. A 'Get that sniper' night-patrol duly materialized. I was amongst those detailed to go on it. The effect this had on me was shocking. My head was full of gory fantasies of lying in the snow bleeding to death. Summer patrols had never affected me so badly. The longed-for change of weather – 'Roll on winter, so we can have a nice rest', we had said all summer – had brought its own problems. As soon as we actually began the patrol I felt much better. And once we left the mule-track the effort of making our way through thigh-deep snow blocked the overflow of my imagination. The sniper's house was right below the Tossignano cliffs but he wasn't at home and nobody else bothered us. As we stomped back to the farm, sweating like pigs, the lines:

'And gentlemen in England, now abed,
Shall hold themselves accurst they were not here,'

flashed into my head.

Would they, I wondered. Would they.

At about eight o'clock on the morning of the day we were due to be relieved – January 13th* – a mortar-bomb blew in the window at one end of the loft. Two other bombs landed up against the back wall. The windiest riflemen ran downstairs in their underwear. The most sanguine – Saddler and the two old soldiers – stayed in bed. Page and I got up, dressed with studied slowness, and went down to investigate the damage. When we opened the back-door we saw that our latrine, boasting a real wooden seat, had received a direct hit.

'They knocked the shit-'ouse down!' shouted Page.

'The poor old shit-'ouse,' he added, and shook his head sorrowfully.

This was a little premature. The seat had not been touched, and we could soon knock up another 'throne'.

We never discovered who had fired the bombs – whether it was our mortar-section, testing for defensive fire, or the enemy. If they had landed half an hour later someone would have been using the

* I kept a sketchy diary during January–March.

latrine, and then the authorities would have had to have held an inquiry.

The march-out was in keeping with the rest of the fortnight. We had only gone a hundred yards when the section's Bren-gunner, one of the old soldiers, fell into a snowdrift. He completely disappeared. All we could see was the imprint of his body and the gun. When we'd dug him out I offered to take over the Bren. He gave it me and made off at speed. Unless I overtook him I would have the Bren for the rest of the march. I soon gave up trying to. The extra weight didn't worry me until we reached a stretch of track running down to the road. The effect of rain on snow, followed by frost and mules, had left it like the Cresta Run. I spent more time on my bottom than my feet. The thought of a nice, flat road was like an oasis. Until I reached it. The snow had melted and then frozen into solid ice. I could get no grip on it at all. I fell around like a novice on an ice-rink. If only someone could film me, I thought. I wouldn't have to worry about what to do after the war. I'd be the new Charlie Chaplin. Then the Company mule-train began to catch me up. The thought of falling under their hooves was a sharp incentive to go faster. The faster I went the faster I fell over. I reached the trucks five yards ahead of the mules.

After a week-end at our country-house we returned to the Line. This time we took over a mountain on the other side of the valley, relieving a tank regiment (they had been turned into infantry, to fill the gap left by the Tossignano battle). The approach march took all day. Monte Penzola, as it was called, has more false crests than any mountain I know. Its real one was as sharp as an arrow, with a dug-out at the point, the rest spread out below it. The ledge connecting the dug-outs was a foot wide. Beneath it lay a drop of sixty feet. The Guards, who had captured Penzola the previous November had lost only one man killed – he had fallen off the ledge.

The night we took over was bitterly cold. Standing guard would be a miserable business. Page and I, who were taking the section's first guard, arranged with the two old soldiers to do six hours on and six hours off, instead of the usual two hours on and two hours off. In this way each party would have a really good sleep.

For a while the enemy entertained us with Spandaus firing tracer at some imaginary target at the foot of their mountain (about a mile away from ours as the crow flies). Then they sent us some shells. The O.P. officer with us promptly rang up his battery. They gave the enemy mountain a light shelling. The enemy gunners stopped firing. So did ours. The war was getting sensible.

During the Christmas rest we had been equipped with winter kit of surprisingly good quality. I had most of mine on – an Arctic vest on top of an ordinary woollen one, two shirts, two pullovers, two pairs of pants, a snow-proof anorak, a greatcoat, a cap-comforter, and a leather jerkin lined and sleeved with an American blanket. The cold got through the lot. When the two old soldiers relieved us we were stiff with it. They had to help us out of the dug-out. Once we reached the 'sleeping' dug-out we revived. The place was like an oven. The tank regiment had left us their primus-stoves. And they had lined the dug-out with American blankets. A mug of tea laced with rum sent me straight off to sleep.

I woke up bathed in sweat. Lovely, I thought, lovely, and dropped off to sleep again. I woke up a second time. The back of my neck felt burning hot. I sat up quickly. Out of the corner of my eye I saw a glow of sparks. Scrambling out of the dug-out – I forgot all about the cliff and nearly fell over it – I tried to stop the smouldering. Thanks to excess clothing my arms flailed about like penguin flippers, and merely sent the sparks flying through the night.

'Put that bloody pipe out!' hissed Saddler.

'I'm on fire!' I hissed back.

'What's up?' said Page, crawling out of the dug-out.

I told him, too, and he dealt with the sparks. Saddler had a look at me.

'There's a hole big enough to put my fist through!' he said. 'How the hell did you do it?'

'I must have gone to sleep with my head on the primus-stove.'

We nearly fell off the ledge laughing. All I had suffered was a burn the size of a sixpence.

Our side of the peak was not under enemy observation. We spent the day sunbathing at the foot of the cliff. 'People would pay to come here in peacetime,' someone remarked.

The enemy avoided us. The peak's forward slope was almost as formidable as the rear one, and they preferred raiding 'A' Company, in a farm on our right, to trying their luck with us. Our first tour on Penzola – it lasted five days – gave us nothing to grumble at.

During a ten-days' rest at our country-house O'Connor fixed me up with a call-girl, an attractive honey-blonde in her early twenties called Angela. She operated from a converted nunnery – I had my leg pulled about that – in Florence. My initiation went well until I mistook her groans of pleasure for pain, and asked if I was hurting her. A. had gone 'on the game' to supplement her 30s. a week wages from A.M.G.O.T. Before she had done so she had spent her evenings helping a friend run an hotel. Americans ate there, and took the waitresses to bed. One evening an American spotted Angela. 'Say, babe,' he'd asked her. 'Do you fuck too?' She had assured him she did not. But it had started her off. She had told her neighbours and landlord that she was going to give painting lessons, and to ensure a well-behaved clientele she insisted that every one should be introduced to her personally. It didn't always work out. One day when we were making love a drunk American hammered on the door. 'If we keep quiet he'll think there's no one here!' whispered Angela. 'Open up, you bitch!' yelled the Yank. 'Or I'll kick the bloody door down!' After several minutes of this he shoved off.

It was during this rest that I had a difference with Saddler. Ever since we had returned to the Platoon Saddler had been gunning for Booth. Poor B. managed to keep clear of him until one particular afternoon. The Platoon were shifting equipment and Booth, carrying some Piat-bombs, walked slap into him. Saddler's pent-up bitterness went off like a bomb. He told Booth he was a clumsy cunt, that but for him Wilson would still be alive. Booth cowered away.

251

Saddler went after him, fists clenched. I got between them. Saddler snarled at me like an animal deprived of its prey. He bawled me out instead of Booth. The venom with which he spoke was hard to stomach, and I made arrangements to get myself transferred to another section (this contained a Geordie, ex-miner, ex-Sunderland F.C. whom I'd hit it off with). Saddler tried to persuade me to change my mind but I thought it better if we gave each other some air.

Towards the end of the rest the Platoon had two leave vacancies – one to Rome, one to Florence. The British leave camp was in a barracks on the outskirts of the city. After checking in I went straight to a flat in the centre – the owners let their spare rooms to servicemen.

I spent most of the leave seeing shows with O'Connor – we liked live variety and thriller films the best – and visiting Angela. I took her flowers, and both of us got all there was to be got out of our relationship. Florence itself did not impress me very much. At no time did I feel in touch with the past (I did later in Siena). I didn't like the Cathedral and I didn't like the girls. They all wore suits tailored from American blankets, but they treated Allied O.R.s as if they'd just crawled out from underneath a stone. I felt like pulling the blankets off them. American aircrews were much more colourful. They walked around in flying-jackets decorated with half-size naked women.

There were lots of tales going the rounds about fights between American and British troops. I shared my flat with a succession of Americans and got on well with them. What trouble there was came about through jealousy. The British top brass always let the American top brass take over the best leave facilities. In Florence, for instance, they had turned the station, bang in the centre of the city, into a leave centre. It was this 'couldn't-care-less' attitude on the part of the British generals, as much as the difference in pay, that caused the bone-head element amongst squaddies to pick fights with Yanks.

One day I walked out of the flat and bumped into half a dozen of them. I took them for Guardsmen until I saw their R.A. badges. They were big, drunk, and cursing Americans.

'Are you a Yank?' one of them demanded, peering at my regimental sidecap.

'No.'

'Well, you're lucky!'

He and his mates staggered on down the stairs. I waited for them to get clear. In the flat above them there were two girls 'on the game'. The Yanks had presumably priced the gunners out of the market. After a couple of minutes I sauntered down the stairs. As I walked out of the front-door two men grabbed me under the arm-pits. Spreadeagled in space I saw a third gunner prepare to deliver a blow that would put *me* out of the market.

'I'm in The Rifles!' I shrieked.

The gunner bent down to examine my regimental cap. He had great difficulty in reading the badge. It was a very small one, an officer's badge, not so easy to read when one was sober. (I wore it because it was silver and looked smarter than the other ranks'.) For an awful moment I thought he wouldn't be able to manage it. He did, though.

'Put him down,' he said.

They put me down, and mouched off in search of the nearest American. A night or so later I came to close-quarters with one myself. The owner of the flat asked me if I would mind sharing my double-bed with one. He was, she assured me, a nice one. I was quite agreeable. The Yank, a dour soul with a bee in his bonnet about American service-women – 'All they come over here for is to get shacked up' – told me he weighed 227 pounds. I weighed 122 myself. I woke up in the middle of the night to find myself on the edge of the bed. The Yank lay beside me fast asleep. I sat up and tried to roll him over. It was like trying to move a large tree trunk. There was only one thing to do. I got out of bed and got in again the other side. I dropped off to sleep again, to wake up on *that* edge. The Yank had simply rolled the other way. I got up and got in the other side. It'll happen a third time, I thought. At any rate it'll make a damn good story. It happened a third time – and a fourth.

The end of my leave coincided with the Company returning from a second trip to Penzola. On February 9th we went back for a nine-day spell. During it a thaw set in. This caused me bouts of intense depression. I usually stopped them by telling myself it was worse in Russia.

At the time I couldn't understand the timing of the depressions. It seems possible that in some primitive unconscious way I managed to 'freeze' my own grief at the death of my friends and of the Battalion itself by identifying with the winter conditions. And once the real thaw set in so my own block melted. Jeffreys and Wilson were dead. O'Connor and Corporal

Bailey were back in England on leave. The skin of courage I had grown in the summer began falling away. The up-and-down swings of life on Penzola imposed its own particular strain. By day we could sunbathe at its foot – someone remarked that people would pay to live that sort of life in peace-time – at night we waited for the, to us, inevitable German fighting patrol. My own dug-out was the most accessible to the enemy. One night I heard stealthy footsteps approaching it from the enemy side. As I tensed with fear someone jumped on top of the dug-out. The shock was so great that my whole body left the duckboard I was lying on. When it returned there I lay waiting to be knifed or clubbed. But nothing happened. Cautiously I looked out of the dug-out. There was no one to be seen. On top of my dug-out lay a lump of mud that must have weighed at least twenty pounds. The footsteps I heard had been smaller pieces falling down the slope above the dug-out, the 'someone' the twenty-pounder. Although this particular shock apparently wore off as quickly as those of the summer it left its mark. When I left the Army after the war any noise at night tended to get me out of bed to try and stop it. One night I got up, dressed, and walked across the road to close a neighbour's swinging gate. Later, when the heat was on psychically noises at night proved a flying start for an anxiety neurosis.

During the day-time depressions I often brooded about having missed the fight at Tossignano. I felt guilty about not having been with the Company. And it had been a battle in which I could have once and for all have found how much courage I really had.

On another night a sniper began taking pot-shots at another of our dug-outs. The O.P. officer pin-pointed his position and another Platoon were told to get him. Half an hour before they set out their officer reported sick with stomach ache. This took courage. I would have preferred to chance the sniper. Another officer had done something rather more spectacular. During a battle he had jumped out of his trench and run. A court-martial would have resulted in the wrong sort of regimental publicity so he had been dumped on us instead. The angle – 'Other ranks run away but officers and gentlemen do not' – grated. As always the officer's reputation arrived before he did. Poor devil, I thought. How'll he face it out? I needn't have worried. He went about things without the slightest trace of shame.

When we descended the mountain we discovered that its last hundred yards had turned into a bog. The mud came up over our knees. A very sharp gradient propelled us forward. The mud held our legs. We toppled into it in slow motion. When we saw one another's faces we rocked with laughter. Until the hail hit us. The stones were big as moth-balls. The storm drove them straight into our faces. As I fell I automatically put the hand shielding my face into the mud. The hail beat into my face until I sobbed. When it stopped – just as we reached the bottom of the track – I let myself go.

Alexander, Churchill, the King – I cussed the lot.

I arrived back at our house feeling very depressed. Arranging with someone to cover me at the next morning's parade I went to Angela. I needed a woman's comfort, even if I had to buy it. Angela told me that she now had an American brigadier in tow. In a few months more she would have made enough money to retire.

During the rest we heard that the next trip to Penzola would be our last. The Division was to be pulled out of the Line for a rest, and to prepare for a spring offensive. But the Battalion was to be disbanded. So as the number would not be lost the 5th were to become the new 3rd. This twisted the knife.

We returned to the mountains knowing that by the time the Division had re-grouped the war might be over. All we had to do was to sit tight on Penzola. The acting C.O. had other ideas. So had the Germans.

They kicked off by ambushing four signallers laying a wire between us and 'A' Company. They then mortared the peak. It wasn't the number – only three bombs each time – that worried us, it was the way they used them. With their first batch they scored a direct hit and a near-miss on one of our O.P. dugouts. With their second they severed the rope we used to pull ourselves up the peak. This, of course, was jammy, but it was the sort of jam that happens to world-beaters. To land a bomb on top of one particular dug-out, using only three bombs from a range of two miles or more, is a fantastic performance. What would they do to Penzola if they felt like it?

Dressing up in the captured signallers' uniform three Germans infiltrated through our lines to a town ten miles behind us. Here one of them blew the gaff by walking into a N.A.A.F.I. and asking for a 'cup of tea, please', instead of a 'cuppa cha'. The N.A.A.F.I. Corporal phoned the military police, and three brave men were shot. The enemy then paid an Italian girl

257

to walk along the valley road and count the guns. The gunners contacted the M.P.s, and they put her in the bag as well. Whilst they were celebrating the girl asked to go to the lavatory. They put a guard on the door but she got away through the window. We loved this.

In the meantime the acting C.O. had been stepping up patrols. The Platoon carried out one two nights before the relief. We had to find out if the enemy were occupying a farm in their half of no-man's land. As if anyone cared.

We had a full moon for the trip. It made me feel quite naked. A lover's moon, I thought, and cursed it.

We were squelching up a gully when a dog began barking. The patrol halted. Word came back confirming the obvious – the dog was in the farm. It had always struck me as strange that neither side made use of watch-dogs. Well, someone *was* making use of one. And it wasn't us.

Another dog began barking. Then a third. By the time we reached a ridge overlooking the farm there were a dozen at it – howling, baying, yelping. What the Germans would be doing with so many dogs didn't enter my head. I was too busy noticing other things. The farm lay under the lee of the enemy's mountains. We had two hundred yards to go. Bare slope. Lit up by the moon like something out of *Son et Lumière*.

Down the slope we went. The dogs greeted us with a frenzy of hate. The Germans held their fire. Making sure they don't miss us, I thought. But what about their pals in the mountains? Why don't *they* open up? At this point fantasy mercifully intervened. Perhaps they've all gone home, I thought. Perhaps the whole bloody Army's packed it in.

As we neared the farm the barking reached a pitch that did for me – at least, I like to think it was the barking. We were in arrow-head formation and I happened to be one of the 'barbs'. If I cared I could drop behind and risk being spotted. This is what I did. (I heard later that the other 'barb' did the same. He was spotted.) When the leading man reached the farm I quickly made up the distance.

All the dogs fled except one. He snarled defiance from just inside the farm.

'Shall I shoot him?' the officer asked me.

As if the dogs weren't enough.

'No, sir.'

Instead the officer unbuttoned his flies and peed into the yard. His innocence – he had never been under fire – fascinated me.

The dog retreated into the bowels of the farm. The officer and an N.C.O. followed it. They soon came out.

'No wonder the dogs didn't like us,' said the officer. 'We've spoilt their dinner. The place is full of dead oxen and dead pigs.'

The officer laid on an ambush. After we'd hung around for twenty minutes a rifleman began seeing Germans.

'Can you see anyone?' the officer asked me.

I couldn't, but I wasn't going to tell *him* that.

'Yessir!' I whispered, pointing at a row of knobbly hummocks.

'I think there's a whole fighting patrol watching us!'

'H'm,' said the officer. 'In that case we'll withdraw a bit.'

After lying up for another hour we returned to spend the rest of the night at Company H.Q.'s farm. Everything in the loft seemed to welcome me back – the grain on which we were lying, the broken furniture, the cobwebs on the roof. The few minutes that elapsed between my getting into my sleeping-bag and going to sleep were charged with intense happiness. We were out of it. Perhaps for ever. Several times I pulled myself back from sleep, reluctant to let it end such a moment, then let it take me like a child.

In the morning we returned to the peak. Major Robins sent us a message. 'In accordance with regimental tradition, i.e. that billets shall be left tidier than when they are taken over, the ox, Penzola, at foot of, shall be buried forthwith.'

The ox had plagued us already. Preserved by frost since its death the previous November it now stank to high heaven.

'If he wants it buried he can come and bury it his fucking self!' said Saddler.

We all seconded this except the officer, who diplomatically suggested that we give it a token burial, and this is what we did. Each of us put one shovel-load of earth on the carcass. Page crowned it with an empty bully-tin.

'Make 'im feel at 'ome,' he said.

The wake took place a fortnight later, on the morning the Battalion was officially broken up.

A dozen of us, including Saddler, Page, Phillips, and Booth met in a wine-bar at 8 a.m. At 11 a.m. it was coming out of our ears.

'Come on, Alec!' shouted Saddler. 'Sing that bloody song of yours!'

I sang 'Come, Landlord fill the flowing bowl' right through. In the middle of one verse I was sick in someone's beret. I went straight on singing, picking the verse up at the exact word I'd left off. The audience loved this.

We broke up at midday. In the open our legs gave way. We had to crawl. All I wanted was to reach the Platoon's open-air latrine. Once on I couldn't get off. I sat there for two hours. Saddler and the rest came to look at me. They went away weak with laughter. There was something very appropriate about it all. Happily I sent the Company on its last parade. The dead and the living swam past me. I took the salute. *E finito, capito? E proprio finito.*

EPILOGUE
RETURN TO MONTE LIGNANO

In July, 1944, the Germans fought a delaying action in the mountains south of Arezzo, in Tuscany. British Intelligence reported an enemy patrol on a Monte Lignano. The infantry company to which I belonged were ordered to clear the mountain. The enemy patrol turned out to be a battalion of Panzer Grenadiers, picked troops in prepared positions. They blew us out of ours. In a two-minute mortar-barrage we lost seven men killed and twenty-six wounded. Our artillery support was smashed to bits by the enemy guns. A stray shell hit a chapel sheltering our wounded. Someone inside began ringing the bell to draw attention to the Red Cross flag on the roof. The German observation officer directed the fire of all his guns – there were over a hundred of them – on to the chapel. Dumb with horror, we watched it struck again and again. Bits flew off the bell-tower. It seemed only a matter of time before the whole building collapsed. We listened to the bell as if our lives depended on it. Slowly the shelling died down. The bell kept ringing. When the shelling stopped it rang faster than ever, echoing and re-echoing in our ears and in our hearts. We were too moved to say anything. If our wounded were all right – and they were, as it turned out – we'd talk about it after the battle.

Next day we were relieved. The enemy guns were bombed. Our own guns softened up the Lignano defences. The New Zealanders were putting in a night attack. Shells and mortar-bombs landed on the mountain at the rate of about twenty a second. It lit up like a penny sparkler. We felt sorry for the Germans. The Kiwis took Lignano with the bayonet.

Battles like Arezzo made me want to write a book about my company. After Slim Brandon was killed I had to write it. During a retreat Slim went back to look for a mortar. The rest of the company huddled together in a clearing – the bushes round it hid us from the enemy. Slim was reported missing. He's had it, someone said. We ignored this. Slim could look after himself. He proved it by suddenly popping out of the bushes, the mortar on his shoulder, one arm raised in a mock-heroic V-sign. We cheered wildly, cheering his spirit, cheering ourselves out of the dumps. As I watched his clowning I felt it wouldn't matter so much if most of us were killed. As long as Slim was around – and I was sure he always would be – he would see to it that we were not forgotten. 'The Germans will never get Slim,' his particular chum said. They didn't. Slim was accidentally shot by his own Bren-gunner. It took me a long time to realize that the job I had earmarked for him was now mine.

I wrote the first draft of the book in 1947. By 1954 I'd written five or six others. None of them was much good. The sentences were strung together and I couldn't remember any dialogue. In 1955 I had a

263

breakdown. I 'heard' shells screaming past my earhole. 88s, by the sound of them. Just like old times. As my world broke up I turned to the one thing I had left to hang on to – my book. I tried another draft. The dialogue came back. I saw the words in my head, just as they'd been spoken. As I scribbled them down I thought of the dead. I owed them so much. I was writing the book for them, for those who were there, and for those who wanted to know what it was like – in that order. At the same time I was trying to forget the dead, to get shot of them. You can't grieve forever. You can't bottle it up either, as I found out one November evening. Judge, my old section commander, had been killed on November 5th, 1944. He'd stepped on a mine designed to explode on impact of over two thousand pounds. It had blown him to bits. One night I dreamt I was walking up the hill where he'd died. A voice shouted, 'There's gold in the hills!' I woke up sensing that the gold was buried grief. I had to dig it up. I painted Judge's body with my pipe next to him. 'You've left part of yourself behind,' someone said. And taken part of Judge with me. I had to let him die. In a paroxysm of grief I saw my subconscious – Judge as Christ crucified, my tears falling round the cross, blowing it up. In place of a cross a willow tree, a child Christ in the branches holding one of my nursery toys – an Easter hen with a nodding head. I painted these images. 'Judge' on the cross turned with a crossless Christ shooting upwards. He didn't take me with Him. I was still earthed with grief. On November 5th, 1957, it exploded. I walked the six miles from Notting Hill Gate to Swiss Cottage, crying the whole way.

I'd avoided re-visiting the battlefields in Italy in case I wandered round feeling sorry for myself as well as the dead. After my big cry I knew this wouldn't happen. In the summer of 1959 I visited the Monte Lignano chapel where our wounded had been shelled. Its stone walls and bell-tower were scarred with shrapnel but it was the roof that interested me. I'd never understood how it had kept out the shells. They went straight through most roofs. The chapel's had inch-thick stone tiles with the usual overlap. No wonder they'd kept the shells out. Some washing hung on a line outside the chapel. A woman came out and asked us if we'd lost our way. I told her about our wounded being in the chapel. I didn't mention the shelling. I hadn't told the friend I was with either. I wasn't sure why. The new owner of the chapel told us that it had been abandoned after the war and she and her family had moved in. We left her collecting the washing and walked over some rough ground behind the chapel, enjoying the sun and the smell of wild peppermint. Suddenly I sensed an extraordinary feeling of peace. It had nothing to do with our physical surroundings. It was the sort of peace you sometimes feel in small country churches. What happened here isn't just a memory, I thought. Our fears for the wounded, our prayers, the bell ringing out across the mountainside, the God in man seeing off the Devil in him – all that had left something in the air as real as the earth we were standing on. Or as real to me. But would it be real to my friend? Did she feel it, too? I waited for her to speak first.

'What a wonderful feeling of peace,' she said.

Then I told her about the shelling.

The next summer I wrote the final draft of my war-book. The only publisher interested – I tried 17 – backed out because he was afraid of being sued for libel.

In 1964 I took a flat in Siena. On the anniversary of the battle of Arezzo I climbed Monte Lignano. I wanted to see the whole battlefield this time. It never occurred to me that the Italian Forestry Commission might have got there first. They'd covered our side of Lignano with conifers. In pouring rain I forced my way through the forest – the trees were only inches apart – hoping to stumble on our old positions. I soon realized that even if I did the trees would prevent me from seeing them. I'd been hoping to look at the trenches and pick up atmosphere. Can't grumble, I thought. You had your ration last time. I pushed on towards the peak. There were no trees on that. In 1944 I'd helped bury the company's dead at the foot of its cliff. The New Zealand dead, and the enemy's, had been buried there, too – and the company's reburied. The Kiwi's support barrage had blown them out of their graves. The War Graves Commission chaps would have dug up all the bodies and reburied them in a military cemetery. I wondered what the German dug-outs would be like. They were usually bigger and deeper than ours. I was in for another surprise. There were no dug-outs on the peak. No dug-outs anywhere. As I stared round in disbelief I realized there were no shell-holes either. Not even a piece of shrapnel. Someone had tidied things up. It must have been the foresters. They'd gone round the battlefield like park-keepers collecting litter, filling in every hole they saw. Time had done the rest. The ground round the peak was as flat and grassy as the rest of the ridge. A casual visitor would never have guessed that men had died there. It was all a bit eerie, in a most unexpected way. I'd been prepared for something in the air, not for the making-good of tidy-minded foresters.

The German side of Lignano was covered with thick scrub. I plunged into it, looking for a path. There didn't seem to be one. I headed for a gully, ducking and weaving past giant brambles, beating them down, showing them who was boss, not caring how much I got scratched. The gully was rocky. I scrambled down small cliffs, enjoying myself. Then the brambles took over. As I bullocked my way through them I suddenly began tiring. Watch it, I thought. The scrub may go on for miles. Better turn back. I did. It took me five minutes to cover a few yards. By then I was exhausted. I'd paced myself for a mountain walk not jungle warfare. I could only tackle the brambles going downhill. Turning round, I forced my way down the gully. The strength drained out of me. I stopped for a second wind. It didn't come. I needed food but I'd eaten my sandwiches hours before. I was soaked to the skin and getting cold. If I flaked out I'd catch pneumonia. The foresters would find my bones and think I had died in the War. You asked for it, chum, I thought. Coming back to the bloody battlefield. Playing silly buggers. Funny in a way. Don't panic. Don't sit down. You'll never get up. Just lifting my arms was an effort. I plucked at the brambles like an old man pruning roses. Each bar seemed harder to tackle than the last. One sprung out of my hands, showing *me* who was boss. I leant against the side of the gully, cursing the bramble. It was shaped like an arc and didn't have any head. None of the brambles had heads. They'd double-rooted themselves back into the earth. They'd root me into it if I wasn't careful. I clawed the bar down, tried to step over it, and tripped. The brambles stopped me from falling. I lay against them like a boxer on the ropes. Can't go on, I thought. I've had it. Then I saw something green. A clearing. The scrub continued on the other side. Perhaps it only went down the mountain and not across it. I tore my way through the last of the brambles and gasped with relief. The clearing was part of the open mountainside. For a moment I stood there drunk with happiness, that same survivor's happiness I'd felt when I left Lignano to the Germans in 1944. Then I strode on down the slope. My strength had come back like a badly-trained dog. I didn't walk back to Arezzo – I marched.

My war-book was published in 1969. The senior librarian at Sandhurst told my publisher he thought that it would become standard reading for anyone studying the Italian campaign. That'll give the book a long life, my publisher said. He was right. The dead would live on in the book. I'd paid my debt.

On Easter Sunday, 1971, I and my ex-wife booked into a hotel in Arezzo. We took a taxi to a shrine in the mountains. On our way back we passed Monte Lignano. I told the driver about the Germans shelling the chapel. God answered your prayers, he said. It had seemed like that.

'Of course you seen the cemetery,' the driver said.

'The cemetery? What cemetery?'

'The *military* cemetery.'

My heart thumped. The past – the one I'd just recreated about Lignano – collapsed. It was going to end differently.

'No,' I said, hoping the anxiety didn't show in my voice. 'I didn't know there was one.'

'Then I take you there – you don't pay! It is beautiful. We of Arezzo, we go there to picnic on Sundays.'

I sat there feeling stunned I'd never thought of finding out if there was a military cemetery near the town. Arezzo had been a biggish battle. The War Graves chaps wouldn't have buried the bodies in some other place. I must have known that. I'd walked over the battlefield thinking of the dead and their temporary graves. Why hadn't I found out where their permanent ones were? Why hadn't I visited them? Because you didn't want to get too close to the dead, I thought. You wanted them buried alive in the book. They're rotting in their graves, chum. You've got to face them there. You've been dodging the column, running away from the pain and guilt of being alive when the best are dead, their lives wasted. Thrown away. For what? A botched civilization. A bitch gone in the teeth. Ezra got it right.

We pulled up outside a high square of hedges with a concrete porch. The sun was coming in low. Even the concrete glowed. There were no cars parked outside, none on the road, nobody about. No houses, just the foothills of Lignano looking particularly beautiful in the evening sunlight.

Miriana and I left the car and walked over to the porch. There was a book of remembrance on a table.

We passed through the porch. And stopped dead. At the far end of the cemetery three poplars swayed in the breeze. The tops bent towards the earth, then flicked back towards the sky. The man who planted them had planted his faith with them. They had become the living crosses he intended. The stone ones were laid out in a hollow square, the open end facing the poplars, with Lignano in the background. If there was a resurrection then this was the way to announce it.

'What a beautiful place,' said Miriana softly.

'I'm going to look for some men I helped bury.'

'I'll wait here.'

She sensed I wanted it that way. If my grief got out of hand I'd douse it. But just as the power and beauty of the poplars had held my eye and lifted my spirit so that atmosphere of the cemetery completely disarmed me. There was no need to get a grip on myself. I was caught up in a diffused sense of joy. It was all round me. I was detached from it. It did not come inside, but it was there for me to share, like a sacrament. I, who'd spent so much of my life grieving for men whose lives had been so pitiably short, who had little time for the 'They shall grow not old as we that are left grow old' approach to those killed in war, who didn't believe in life after death in any orthodox sense – I found myself thinking: 'They gave their lives and God gave them joy. It's here, all round me. Perhaps that's what resurrection means. The spirit of man living on after him, in the ground and in the air. Preserved and nourished by the sun.'

I found the graves near the poplars. The ages of the dead men ranged from 18 to 20. Five of the crosses were marked 'Known only to God'. That brought a lump to my throat. One of the five had been the last of six brothers. All the others had been killed in the War. I'd thought of his mother then and I thought of her now. I wished I could have gone back to England and told her about the atmosphere in the cemetery. Coming from me it might have helped. But I no longer remembered the rifleman's name. He wasn't from my platoon. I glanced along the line of crosses. They were all carved with the regimental badge. I walked slowly past them. Most of the dead belonged to another battalion. Then I saw the name of our Company pay-clerk, aged 19. Everyone had liked him except those after his job. Pay-clerks didn't go into action. A stray shell had got him. We'd been well North of Arezzo by then. The dead came from a wider area than I'd realised. I walked on warily. It was like being on patrol again, only this time I was afraid of names instead of Germans. I saw Captain Ede's. I stared at his cross, intensely aware of what he had meant to the company and to me. He'd held us together on Lignano. When I heard he'd been killed I felt as if someone had hit me on the chest with a hammer. My sense of loss was still sharp. But I could no longer think of his life as being wasted. I moved on, not really knowing what to think. Suddenly I was facing 'Judge's' grave. All my images had come to dust. 'Judge' was bones beneath my feet. But not just bones. Perhaps I hadn't been dodging the column after all. Perhaps something had kept me from the cemetery until it was time for me to come. For just as he had helped me face death so now 'Judge' and the rest of the dead were helping me

271

place it.

I didn't find Slim's grave. When I went back to see if his name was in the book of remembrance I found that half the pages were torn out. One way of getting a souvenir. It was time to go.

'Did you find the graves?' Miriana asked.

'Yes. Some of my friends in the book, too.'

Perhaps one day I'd write one about survivor's luck.